# The Essence of Modern Haiku

*Photo by Hashimoto Shōkō*
*Cover design by Ashizawa Kazuko and Hidaka Miki*
*Cover calligraphy by Hidaka Keisen*
*Illustrations by Ashizawa Kazuko and Hidaka Miki*

Distributed in the United States by Weatherhill, Inc.
300 Long Beach Boulevard
Stratford, Connecticut 06497-7116.

Distributed in Japan by Sekai Shuppan Kenkyū Centre
2-18-9 Minami-Aoyama, Minato-ku
Tokyo 107

*Published by Mangajin, Inc.*
*Box 6668, Marietta, Georgia 30065*

Printed in the United States of America
First edition

ISBN 0-9634335-0-4
ISBN 0-9634335-3-9 (pbk)

*In memory of Kodaira Keiji*

# *Contents*

## 300 Poems by Yamaguchi Seishi

*Note:* Japanese name order (surname followed by given name) has been used except on the cover and title page.

# *Foreword*

Yamaguchi Seishi is a poet who broke like a cyclone on the world of the new haiku founded by Shiki and Kyoshi. That fact has been made abundantly clear by the authors of this book.

His subjects are fresh. His style is organized and plastic. The feeling of his poetic expression is above all modern. For these reasons, lovers of haiku and lovers of art everywhere would find themselves in tune with Seishi's haiku.

In 1988, Fujiwara Noboru published *A Selection from the Poems of Seishi*, which introduced 88 poems, with the poet's notes, in English translation. We are now given 300 of the poems in English, all selected and annotated by the poet—valuable aids in the comprehension of the poems, needless to say.

Of course, the two distinguishing features of the haiku are its brevity and the tight music of its seventeen sounds. A little longer and it becomes verbose; a little shorter and it loses its rhythm.

Consequently, the principal problem of translating haiku comes down to a matter of the paucity of vowels, and thus syllables, in the English word. When one attempts to translate into seventeen English syllables, one is apt to be forced to conflate the meaning of the Japanese.

R. H. Blyth has suggested a meter of alternating feet in a 2-3-2 rhythm, which seems to satisfy the rhythmic requirements of speakers of English. Poets in Europe and the United States, however, often compose in syllabic patterns close to those of the Japanese, and even the renowned English poet James Kirkup goes on writing poems with the 5-7-5 beat.

Let us remember, too, that nowadays musicians in Europe and the United States are being drawn to the subtle rhythms of *gagaku* and the *shakuhachi*.

With all this in mind, the translation of haiku into English poems of seventeen syllables might be said to have a startlingly new quality.

Thus the work of Kodaira Takashi and Alfred H. Marks seems to me to have been very successful. The translation of the poems and of the annotations is faithful, and the rhythmic quality is sensitively reproduced.

Thanks to this book, therefore, the poems of Yamaguchi Seishi of which Japanese are so proud can be properly appreciated abroad. I anticipate that this will do much for the understanding of haiku in general.

UCHIDA SONO
President, Haiku International Association

# Preface

The haiku has risen to a position of considerable stature in the world. Its name has made its way into many languages, and poems imitating the Japanese haiku are composed just about everywhere. The interest is particularly strong in the United States, where translations and original haiku in English appear even in elementary school textbooks and pupils are encouraged to write them. Over 70,000 haiku were submitted from 27 countries for the Japan Airlines haiku contest early in 1992.

Donald Keene, one of the foremost figures in the study of Japanese literature in English, said a few years ago, in a lecture at the Shiki Museum in Matsuyama, that readers of poetry outside Japan now want to read and study modern haiku, rather than those composed by great masters of the past like Bashō and Buson, with which they have long been familiar. Nevertheless, modern haiku are not available to them. This volume has been prepared to reverse some of that deficiency. It presents translations of 300 haiku of Yamaguchi Seishi (1901- ) a poet who has been active in the composition and publication of haiku in Japan for much of the twentieth century.

Translation of poetry is always difficult, particularly when the work being translated is a literary classic. The effects that brought the work reverence in one language often do not come over in another language. The words fail. They must often be supplemented through skillful incorporation of relevant parts of the larger literary tradition and frequently by annotation. The volume that follows is therefore the product of a somewhat elaborate translation strategy, a strategy the translators have plotted over the past quarter-century of their association, much of which has been taken up with discussions of literature in general and haiku in particular. The decision to collaborate on the translation of the haiku of Yamaguchi Seishi began about four years ago.

The aim from the beginning was to carry into the translations as much of the flavor of the Japanese as possible, while also entertaining with good poetry. The most satisfactory text for translation seemed to be the *Selected Poems of Yamaguchi Seishi*, which had been issued under the sponsorship of the Association of Haiku Poets, in 1979, as part of its *Haiku with Notes by Authors* series. Its 300 poems are highly representative of Seishi's verse, and the valuable poet's notes accompanying each poem promised to simplify greatly the task of interpretative commentary. Permission was therefore secured, from the publisher and the poet.

The strategy for presenting the poems required much more thought. The haiku's outwardly simple pattern of 5-7-5 syllables is not nearly so simple to translate as it seems, particularly against the background of the past century or so of translation of haiku into English. In the first place, Japanese syllables are not the same as those of English. Second, poetry in English has no native form made up of three short unrhymed lines with no regular rhythmic pattern. The closest parallels, indeed, are blank verse, with a specified line length and beat but no rhymes; the epigram (a short witty statement, frequently rhyming) and the aphorism (a terse statement in prose). In fact, judging by the poems printed in probably the most influential magazine presenting haiku in English—meaning the Haiku Association of America's *Frogpond*—practicing haiku poets composing in English have pretty much given up on the 5-7-5 pattern and turned to one that consists of three lines of free verse, with a total of fewer than seventeen English syllables. Some of that movement away from the traditional Japanese form may indeed have been inspired by earlier action by a few Japanese poets.

Undaunted, we have chosen to translate in a pattern of 5-7-5 English syllables. Translation in any other pattern seemed to us to be ignoring one of the principal qualities of Seishi's verse. Just about all the poems we were translating, after all, observe the conventions of 5-7-5. Not only that, if we wanted to translate into free verse we would more properly have turned to the poetry of Kawahigashi Hekigotō (1873-1937), Taneda Santōka (1882-1940), or Ozaki Hōsai (1885-1926), famous for their variations from the norm. Seishi, however, even though he is many ways a revolutionist, seldom departs from the rhythmical norm, and translating his poems in a way that would make him seem to be varying consistently from that basic element of Japanese verse seemed to us to be unwise.

A small number of the poems in the volume being translated, however, do vary from the 5-7-5 pattern. One is poem 29, which the poet labels in his note as having "broken meter." At times, also, the phrasing of the poem shows clearly that the poet has placed a polysyllabic word across the place where two lines normally separate. The Japanese call the practice *kumatagari* —literally "line straddling"—meaning enjambment. If the peculiar conditions that forced the variation in Japanese are translatable, we have rendered them in the English version. Otherwise, we have adhered to the norm.

A property of the haiku that is probably even more important—and more translatable—than the rhythmic pattern is its association with nature. The haiku is, above all, a nature poem, expected to present an event taking place in one of five seasons (New Year's is the fifth). Those seasonal events are rather closely controlled—as is so common in other pursuits in Japan—by senior colleagues working loosely through associations, meetings, and respected publications. Important haiku that have been written in the past and the subjects they present are selected, classified and codified by master haiku poets and printed in almanacs called *saijiki*, or "year-time-record," where they are indexed by words and phrases known as *kigo*, or "season words." Just about every haiku written in Japanese is built around a season word. This word, or phrase, refers the reader to the season concerned and a definite topic within that season as the Japanese have experienced it in the past. The words are broadly classified under: celestial phenomena, topography, holiday observances, life, animals (including insects), plants, and the season itself. Words and topics cover, however, only a narrow range of subjects in traditional Japanese culture. That is one of the reasons for the *saijiki*: to keep the poetry manageable by assigning and classifying, under the authority of tradition, the words to be used with each season. Thus association of word to season is not always what the person new to Japanese haiku would expect. The moon, for instance, is associated with autumn, the moon-viewing season. Insects also tend to call up autumn, though the butterfly is a spring animal. Nevertheless cherry blossom poems are predictably for spring, mountain climbing poems for summer, red leaves for autumn, and snow poems for winter.

Japanese poets depend upon and often carry with them pocket-sized *saijiki,* which assist them to compose within the tradition established by other haiku poets, of all times. Their readers are often conversant with the almanacs and even the season words in them and judge poems by their adherence to or subtle variation from what they know has been done before.

Yamaguchi Seishi became Editor in charge of classification for *Hototogisu* magazine in 1927 and has written extensively on the subject of the *saijiki*. Many of his poems are cited in the *saijiki* in print and often have received special attention. The seasonal aspects of Seishi's poems have, therefore, been treated with great respect in the translations in this volume, representing, as they do, part of the tradition that lies behind the haiku.

The translators have labored to present the poems before them with the seasonal elements of the haiku in mind, in order to help the reader to see the rules of the haiku word game, to watch the poet inch into composition with his season word prepared— perhaps after consulting a *saijiki*—and building his thoughts around that season word in phrases of 5-7-5 to produce his poem. The season word of every poem has been identified and classified. Every effort has been made to make each translation work in tune with the limitations imposed on haiku by established seasonal conventions.

The project has most recently been blessed by affiliation with what is surely one of the outstanding purveyors of bilingual publishing in the world, *Mangajin*. Its peerless editorial staff has not only held the translators up to new, higher standards of performance, but has also helped with annotation of the poems in such a way as to make the process of composition and translation of the haiku perhaps clearer than it has ever been before. Thanks to those notes many haiku poets who know little Japanese will undoubtedly be able to compose translations that will rival those in this book, and we wholeheartedly wish them well.

ALFRED H. MARKS

# Acknowledgments

This volume would not have been completed without the assistance of many people, only a few of whom we have the space to mention and the wit to thank adequately.

First, we are proud to say, is Yamaguchi Seishi himself, who after granting permission for the translation of *Selected Poems of Seishi Yamaguchi* (The Association of Haiku Poets), gave generously of his time to answer questions we have had from time to time, exhibiting qualities of heart and soul we shall never forget.

We are particularly grateful, also, to the Chief Director of the Association of Haiku Poets, Kusama Tokihiko, with whom we conferred as we set out on this task, and to Nakajima Hiroyo, who gave us guidance and assistance with our research on Yamaguchi Seishi. We also thank Uchida Sono, President of the Haiku International Association, for his kind Foreword.

In applying for and securing a Joint Project Grant from the International Studies Committee of Yokohama City University in 1989, the Ministry of Education, Science and Culture International Travel Grant in 1990, and the Ministry of Education, Science and Culture Grant-in-Aid for Scientific Research (Grant-in-Aid for Publication of Scientific Research Results) in 1992, we have received much encouragement from officials at the Yokohama City University, namely: Nakayama Hirokuni, Ōta Yoshio, and Uchiyama Hiromi, whom we thank heartily. We are also grateful to President Takai Shūdo and Dean Itō Ryūji of the Yokohama City University and to Vice President William Vasse and Dean Marleigh Ryan of the State University of New York at New Paltz for granting each of us visiting professorships and making us welcome at their institutions as we conferred for long periods in each other's stamping grounds.

We have appreciated much the interest and the favors of the Association of Haiku Poets and the Ministry of Education, Science and Culture throughout the project.

We also thank Virginia Murray and Wayne Lammers for their editing and annotation of the manuscript and seeing the book through the press; Hashimoto Shōkō, for his stunning photograph; and Vaughan P. Simmons, Editor-in-Chief and Publisher of *Mangajin*, for his close supervision of all the publishing details.

Without the devoted encouragement of esteemed college friends of one of us, namely Kimura Akira and Inoue Keizō, this volume would never have seen the light of day. Finally, we thank Moteki Hiromichi, of *Mangajin*. Without his faith in what we were doing our publication plans would not have come to fruition.

To these and the many others who have helped us and whom we have not named we are eternally grateful.

# A Study on Yamaguchi Seishi

## 1. His Modernity

In his celebrated work *The Beginnings of Modern Haiku*, Azuma Kyōzō writes: "One cannot emphasize too much that contemporary haiku began with Yamaguchi Seishi and his works." Let us begin by analyzing Yamaguchi's contemporaneity.

In the Foreword to Seishi's maiden collection, *Frozen Harbor*, Takahama Kyoshi—Seishi's mentor—wrote: "In his haiku the poet moves into areas unheard of in the past; he carries his halberd into the frontier. His criticism, furthermore, has a preciseness that gives evidence of a very individual viewpoint in the present haiku world." When we enquire into that advance "into the frontier," however, we come up with provocative answers.

Seishi seeks material for haiku not only in nature but also in the works of man. Although Shiki thought of railway trains, for instance, to be unfit for haiku, Seishi composed:

> Up to summer grass,
> wheels of a locomotive
> coming to a stop. *(23)*

He has turned to new and modern materials for haiku, expanding the subject matter throughout the great concerns of urban life: industrial processes, dockyards, steamships, skating rinks, hotels, dance halls, courtrooms, elevators, whaling ships, swimming pools, even Christmas.

Look at some examples from the pages that follow:

> A row of awnings—
> darkness settles down upon
> the movie district. *(7)*

> Smelting furnaces,
> flush up against high mountains
> verdant with July. *(8)*

> Even in the time
> it takes to tie on ice-skates,
> the heart beats faster. *(18)*

> The sound of the gun
> rebounding from the surface
> of hard pool water. *(38)*

Through poems like these he has not only expanded the scope of the materials of haiku; he has also made haiku modern. Seishi shattered long ago the tradition of "singing the birds and flowers," and said goodbye to the lyrical haiku of the past. A salient illustration of this is:

> The summer river
> immersing the scarlet end
> of an iron chain. *(39)*

That crisp, hard poem is practically a touchstone of modern haiku, and very typical of Seishi, to whom the essence of haiku is juxtaposition—the juxtaposition of objects. When he composes, he juxtaposes seasonal material with other material. It is a process quite similar to what C. D. Lewis described in *Poetic Image*: "The process by which this host of images creates a poem is one of conflict—the second image will 'contradict the first,' and so on." Lewis was talking about the way in which many images go together to make a poem, and how in the most basic cases the images collide. Thus the combination of two images may be seen as the smallest unit of poetry. That is haiku.

In the brief space of 5-7-5 sounds, the collision of many images would be chaotic; thus the restriction to one season word. Two season words make for "season surplus" (*kikasanari*), which is unpleasant. Thus, the haiku is born from the abrupt meeting of the image of the season word with one other image. This is referred to as "Two phrases, one poem" (*niku isshō).

Normally, the 5–7–5 pattern of the haiku breaks down either into 5 and then 7–5, or 5–7 and then 5. Two independent phrases, one of which is the season phrase, go together to make one poem. An example of each may be cited from the volume that follows:

> A frozen harbor—
> what was once a Russian town
> there and nothing more. *(3)*

> Solitary bay
> with the tide quieting down—
> a cricket chirping. *(117)*

Of course, Bashō said of haiku: "It may have only one object." ("*Ichibutsu no ue ni naki mono ni arazu.*" [*Travel Sleep Essay*]) Seishi agrees. Take, for instance:

> The firefly's light
> is green in the period
> when it is brightest. *(285)*

The blue fire of the firefly's light is combined here with a green fire. In describing images like this, Seishi used the term *kussetsu*, meaning something like "refraction." In short, through a process of refraction the blue is transformed into green. In a broad sense this can be termed: "Two phrases, one poem."

Doesn't what we are talking about here fit well with the tradition of T. E. Hulme, the Imagists, and T. S. Eliot? What T. E. Hulme enunciated in "Romanticism and Classicism" was taken up by the Imagist poets in *Some Imagist Poets* (1915) and their "Manifesto":

1. To use the language of common speech, but to employ always the exact word, not the nearly-exact, nor the merely decorative word.
2. To create new rhythms . . .
3. To allow absolute freedom in the choice of subject.
4. To present an image.
5. To produce poetry that is hard and clear, never blurred or indefinite.
6. Finally . . . concentration is the very essence of poetry.

And this is, is it not, close to the definition of haiku we have been discussing? Related to it are T. S. Eliot's words in his essay "Hamlet and His Problems":

> The only way of expressing emotion in the form of art is by finding an objective correlative. . . such that when the external facts, which must terminate in sensory experience, are given, the emotion is immediately evoked.

And just as Eliot made every effort to find the objective correlative, so Seishi has labored at the juxtaposition of two objects, and to express himself through them, through things.

In juxtaposition, intellect works. Seishi expresses this with the word *kōsei*, meaning "composition." He said: "The method of my poetry is the composition of a sketch from nature" ("Before a Poem is Made" [*Ikku no naru made*]). This means that, by constructing intellectually the reality of a sketch from nature, one transforms the real world into the world of art. No words on this approach are more apt than those of Kyoshi, cited earlier: "His criticism . . . has a preciseness that gives evidence of a very individual viewpoint in the present haiku world." His intellect makes songs out of the juxtapositions in haiku. As Seishi, to whom creation and criticism are one, sees it, criticism can never surpass creation and creation cannot surpass criticism. Like Eliot, Seishi is a master of creation and criticism.

But what does it mean to say that poems are born from the collision of two

juxtaposed images? In his "The Hannya Sutra and the Principles of Association,"
[*Hannya Shingyō to Rensō Hiyakuhō*] Seishi begins with the words of Mallarmé:
"Since objects are already in existence, it is not necessary to create them. All we
have to do is grasp the relationships among them." The same is true of haiku. The
landscape architect doesn't simply bring this stone into juxtaposition with that
stone. He brings the vital part of this stone into juxtaposition with the vital part of
that stone. Similarly, the good haiku brings the vital aspect of one object into
juxtaposition with the vital aspect of another object. Thus:

> In the cold garden,
> they really should have left out
> more of the stones! *(179)*

A little more on "The Hannya Sutra," known outside Japan by the name
*Saddharma Pundarika Sutra*. In that work, two very important concepts are
emptiness *[Kū]* and karma *[In'en]*. Emptiness refers to the way things are constantly
locked in change. Restlessly changing objects, caught by karma, move into
relationships with other changing objects, all the while continuing to change. While
taking hold of the present moment, haiku must grasp with the eyes of the spirit the
invisible relationships existing among objects lost in time and space—

> Dunes in a cold wind—
> the shape they take before me,
> the shape of today. *(151)*

Seeing with the spirit is taken up early in "The Hannya Sutra" in the words *kan
jizai bosatsu*, meaning that the Buddhist saint, or Bodhisattva, sees readily with the
eyes of the spirit. One whose imagination is perfectly free in time and space is able
to see the relationships between things. Thus Seishi moves easily in both Christian
and Shintō subjects:

> The Lord's hands and feet,
> with the nails hammered through them—
> dewdrops on blossoms. *(9)*

and:

> Moving the great shrine—
> under the eternal eye
> of the Cygnus stars. *(268)*

The orientation of Seishi's haiku is principally Buddhist. Yet they are all thoroughly
modern.

## 2. His Place in Haiku History

Seishi was born in 1901, and he is still active among haiku poets, still in the forefront. He was a student of Takahama Kyoshi (1874–1959), one of the "twin stars" among the students of Masaoka Shiki (1867–1902), the greatest master of modern haiku. The other star was Kawahigashi Hekigotō (1873–1937). Seishi continues, however, as the others did in their time, to pay homage to the peerless Matsuo Bashō (1644–1694).

Seishi said in "The Words of Bashō": "My haiku are entirely in the tradition of Bashō." That tradition, he explained, came to him through Shiki, Kyoshi—who succeeded Shiki as publisher of the periodical *Hototogisu*—and Hekigotō. Kyoshi wrote what Shiki considered to be the three essential components of haiku: sketching from nature (*shasei*), objective description (*kyakkan byōsha*), and juxtaposition (*haigō*) in his "Six–Month Course in Haiku." Let us look at those three elements as Shiki thought of them.

When Shiki said, "represent nature" in "Haiku in the 29th Year of Meiji," (1896) he was isolating sketching from nature as a basic ingredient of haiku. And of objective description, he clarified: "It does not mean description of the feelings evoked by objectivity, but the objective description of objects, and through them the stimulation of the emotions of the reader" (*Principles of Haiku*). From those words we can see how emotions may be expressed through things.

Juxtaposition, finally, must be carried out in combination with the season. Shiki said: "Make a poem . . . by bringing the season together with one of the myriad of subjects outside the season" (*Principles of Haiku*). And also: "The seasonal subject must elicit associations of the season . . . From those associations one can begin to call forth in 17 syllables the limitless nuances of earth and sky" (*Principles of Haiku*). From this we can see how Shiki favored the combination of seasonal objects with associated objects. The cardinal importance of juxtaposition for him is expressed in the words: "Through juxtaposition antitheses are harmonized" ("Haiku in Search of a 'Hand'"). Thus Shiki favored haiku which are approached as sketches from nature, which contain juxtaposition, and which are objectively presented.

However, this was very much what Bashō said. In *The Three Notebooks* and *Travel Sleep Essay*, edited by Bashō's disciples, we can learn more about "sketching from nature." In *The Three Notebooks*, we read: "The changes of heaven and earth are the seeds of literature." For heaven and earth, read "nature," and for literature, read "haiku." "Before the light that things give off dies in the heart, it must be expressed" (*The Three Notebooks*). Thus we must observe nature and record its changes.

For more on objective description, let us look at the statement: "From the colors of the mind in thought, transformed into objects, the shape of the poem is decided"

(*The Three Notebooks*). The "colors of the mind in thought" are the images received from nature. They are "transformed into objects" as the impressions of nature become the words for things. Thus the form of the poem evolves, and thus we can understand how, to Bashō, the form of the poem is arrived at as the impressions of nature become the words for things.

Finally let us take up juxtaposition. Bashō said in *The Three Notebooks*: "Look at *hokku* as something brought together." In *Travel Sleep Essay,* he said: "Things brought in from the outside provide an ageless source of poems." From these statements we can understand how Bashō, like Shiki, advised juxtaposition through association. Bashō's "the bringing together of melancholy things with less than melancholy things" (*Travel Sleep Essay*) and the words quoted earlier from Shiki, "Through juxtaposition antitheses are harmonized," are very similar statements, are they not?

In this way, Shiki was a bona fide literary heir to Bashō. And what about Kyoshi? He inherited two of Shiki's three principles, the sketch from nature and objective representation, and emphasized them in his terms "singing the birds and flowers" and "objective sketching from nature," using them to lead the way for some excellent disciples. In the section entitled "Haiku" in his *The Road to Haiku*, he named the first chapter "Objective Sketching from Nature," and the second chapter "Singing the Birds and Flowers." His failure to discuss juxtaposition makes clear how much he valued the other two principles.

In "On New Directions in Haiku," by Kyoshi's contemporary Kawahigashi Hekigotō, however, we can read that: "Sketching from nature is not the ultimate objective of poetry composition." It was important to Hekigotō but not the "ultimate." Another vital objective is imagination *[sōka],* and he went on to say: "Look at things as if karma is involved and combine them subjectively." From this we can understand why he emphasized sketching from nature and combination. Thus *Hekigotō* inherited two of Bashō's principles, sketching from nature and juxtaposition, and leaned toward free haiku.

Seishi said: "I have inherited the entire legacy of Kyoshi and Hekigotō and stand by the sketch from nature, juxtaposition, and objective representation. My haiku are entirely in the tradition of Bashō" ("The Words of Bashō"). Bashō is the progenitor, Shiki the parent who rebuilt the dynasty, and Seishi the legitimate heir to the traditional haiku.

## 3. His Haiku

In 1991, Seishi and the twentieth century were 91 years old. He has continued to compose; to manage the monthly periodical *Tenrō*; to go through 10,000 poems a week for the *Asahi Newspaper* haiku column; to give weekly lectures at the Asahi Cultural Center as well as the Hankyū and Academy haiku classes; to lead monthly haiku conferences in Tōkyō, Nagoya, and Ōsaka; and to continue advising his disciples. His instructional scheme continues to follow the three principles: sketching from nature, juxtaposition, and objective representation. It also adheres to standard Japanese language and the 5–7–5 pattern.

Let us analyze some of the poems in the volume that follows using suggestions from Seishi's "My Principles; My Thoughts on Haiku":

1. Omission:

> Rodin would have trimmed
> these soaring cumulus clouds,
> with their excess flesh. *(313)*

Seishi found Rodin's advice about the breadth and the depth of sculpture useful in creating haiku. Like the sculpture Rodin described, the poem must have depth as well as breadth; depth and breadth work together. The seventeen syllables supply the breadth; the meanings compressed in that tight space supply the depth. Seishi thought Rodin would have found nature guilty of overstatement in those broad cumulus clouds.

2. Relationship:

> The iron framework
> twisted in a moment's time
> bleaches in the cold. *(177)*

Here the present wintry moment with the Hiroshima wreckage is combined with the past summery moment of the bomb explosion. The two widely separated but closely related points of time are brought together by a highly intellectual technique called "abstract structure" [*chūshō kōsei*].

3. Metaphor:

> A mountain hollow,
> becoming a sniffing bowl
> for mikan blossoms. *(170)*

In the presence of nature, the imaginative power operates, producing, by an associational leap, a metaphorical haiku. Dialectically, we are given thesis, antithesis, and synthesis. The thesis leaps to the antithesis to produce metaphor.

4. Word Blend:

> Hand-held sparkler
> gushing fiery bubbles—
> fire is water. *(314)*

The compound word must be handled with great care, lest the poem become overloaded. The Japanese word for sparkler, *Te-hana-bi*, is a condensation of *te ni motsu hanabi*, "hand-held-flower-fire." The word *tehanabi* was coined by Seishi. The Japanese sparkler, incidentally, is dangled by a string, between the hand and the ground.

> 5.  Season word:
>
>     Holy of holies—
>     where the stupas of the dead
>     become snow fences. *(197)*

"Snow fence" is the season word in this haiku. It is a compound word with great energy that blends words and meanings, as well as time and space. When the season word collides with another locution in this way, sparks fly.

Thus, by his powers of expression, Seishi produces 17-syllable poems with more than seventeen syllables of meaning. One can compare them with the work of Western artists like those already referred to—T. S. Eliot, C. D. Lewis, and Stéphane Mallarmé—and others like T. E. Hulme, Ezra Pound, Amy Lowell, and H. D., among the Imagists, as well as artists like Wallace Stevens, Rainer Maria Rilke, Pierre Charles Baudelaire, Paul Valery, Ernest Hemingway, Sergei Michailovich Eisenstein, Auguste Rodin, Vincent Van Gogh, and Pablo Picasso.

Many have pointed out the undeniable effect on Yamaguchi Seishi of his family problems. He was placed in the care of his maternal grandparents in his second year, and two of his sisters were placed in the homes of other families. He was nine when his mother committed suicide. Pulmonary illnesses of varying degrees of seriousness dogged him for thirty of his younger years, forcing him to take leave for a time from his studies at the Imperial University of Tōkyō, and reoccurring at the time he was employed by the Sumitomo Corporation.

Let us say more about the effect on him of World War II. All the haiku poets suffered during that conflict. Some were jailed: Hirahata Seitō, Saitō Sanki and Akimoto Fujio, all of whom worked on *Tenrō* after the war. Some of them, like Hino Sōjō, escaped arrest but stopped writing. But what happened to Seishi? As the standard bearer of the generation of rising poets, and a prime target for repression, he was constantly singled out by the authorities. Perhaps it was his illness that saved him.

He escaped arrest, but concern over the future of his country followed him to his sickbed. The war threw a dark shadow over him. Some of that shadow may be seen in the following two haiku:

> A cricket peering
> intently into regions
> subterranean. *(46)*

> Once over the sea,
> winter winds can no longer
> return home again. *(80)*

Seishi's haiku are square and dignified, and are reputed to be deficient in color and brilliance. In fact, at first glance, they are marked by a dark, leaden quality:

> Karafuto's sky
> lowering—the arrival
> of schools of herring.

But not all of his haiku are like that. Take:

> Spring has come again,
> with week after glorious week,
> each of seven days. *(51)*

And:

> Up into the sky
> a penetrating azure—
> red spider lily. *(55)*

Seishi himself, in the preface to *Frozen Harbor*, said:

I am not exaggerating when I say the tremendous start given to *Hototogisu* over the past ten years was brought about by the activities of two groups of intelligentsia: first, the Third High School and Kyōto University Haiku Conference led by Messrs. Suzuka Noburo and Hino Sōjō, and, second, the University of Tōkyō Haiku Conference led by Shūōshi.

My haiku were formed in the Third High School and Kyōto University conference, and made their debut in the University of Tōkyō conference. I consider myself to be unusually blessed by circumstances.

That is what he said, but when one considers this amazing human being and his splendid beginning and his progress thereafter, one might consider with profit a work by another man. It is "The Table," by André Derain.

Derain, Henri Matisse and Maurice de Vlaminck were the best known painters of France's efflorescent Fauvism. Under the influence of Vincent Van Gogh and Paul Gauguin, early Fauvism developed bright, even flashy, coloring. Later, however, Derain and his group were attracted by Pablo Picasso and other cubists, and this new influence may be seen in Derain's austere, monochromatic, geometric productions. They stand in striking contrast to his earlier Fauvism. "The Table" is the epitome of firm construction. Seishi, too, has that talent for firm construction.

> Voices in the fog,
> voices assuming a shape—
> the shape of a school. *(160)*

> Day to remember
> Bashō—wall of a building,
> precipice of glass. *(243)*

Half of "The Table" is black; the rest is blue, dark brown, and gray. Brilliant tones are absent. And yet there is a certain charm to it. It is, without doubt, inimitably Seishi. "The Table" is a work that has the stamp of Seishi—avatar of the new-age haiku.

The following words by Takahashi Kenji sum up the achievement of Yamaguchi Seishi:

> When Seishi came, the haiku took a turn of 180 degrees. He accomplished, literally, a Copernican revolution. Into our new haiku world, new members are rising like a cloud. Yet almost none of them would be there were it not for the existence of Seishi ("On Yamaguchi Seishi").

These sentences were written about 60 years ago. Yet Yamaguchi Seishi has continued to flourish as the leader of the haiku world, a fact which was underscored as recently as November 1992, by the action of the Japanese government in naming him among fifteen recipients of the Award for Cultural Merit.

KODAIRA TAKASHI

# Chronology

1901    Born November 3 (5 in family register), first child of Yamaguchi Shinsuke and Mineko, residing in Fukunokawa, Okazaki-chō, Kamikyō-ku, Kyōto. Named Chikahiko.

1908    **April.** Enters Kinrin Elementary School.

1909    **Autumn.** Takes up residence with his maternal grandfather, Wakita Kaichi, in Sendagaya-mura, Toyotama-gun, Tōkyō. Transferred to Masago Elementary School.

1911    Grandfather Wakita sails for Karafuto to become General Manager of the *Karafuto Nichinichi Shinbun*.
        **June.** Mother, Mineko, commits suicide.

1912    **July.** Joins his grandfather in Karafuto, and transfers into the Toyohara Elementary School.

1914    **April.** Enters the Ōdomari Middle School. Develops a passion for the traditional haiku, thanks to instruction from Nagai Teppei, instructor in Japanese language.

1917    **April.** Leaves Karafuto and returns to Kyōto, where he transfers into the Kyōto First Middle School.

1919    **July.** Enters the second department of liberal arts of the Third High School.

1920    **October.** Takes part in the Kyōto Imperial University and Third High School Haiku Conference. Receives direction from Hino Sōjō and Suzuka Noburo. Submits a poem to *Hototogisu* and signs poem with alternate characters for the name Chikahiko.

1922    **March.** In Kyōto, first meets Takahama Kyoshi, who reads the name with the new characters and pronounces it Seishi.
        **April.** First meets Mizuhara Shūōshi.
        **April.** Enters the law department of the Imperial University of Tōkyō.
        **April.** With Mizuhara Shūōshi, Tomiyasu Fūsei, and others, revives the University of Tōkyō Haiku Conference.

1924    **October.** Weighed down by pleurisy, drops out of college.

1926    **March.** Graduates from the law department of the Imperial University of Tōkyō.
        **April.** Goes to work in the Sumitomo Main Office.

1928    **June.** Maternal grandfather dies.
        **October.** Marries Asai Umeko (pen name Hatsujo), oldest daughter of

Asai Yoshiteru (pen name Teigyo) and Masa. They set up housekeeping at Saishōyama, Higashi-ku, Ōsaka.

1929 **November.** Meets Hashimoto Takako and Hirahata Seitō for the first time.
**December.** Promoted to the governing board of *Hototogisu.*

1932 **May.** Publishes his first book of haiku: *Frozen Harbor [Tōkō]* (Sojinsha Books).

1935 **February.** Publishes second book of haiku: *Yellow Flag [Kōki]* (Ryūseikaku).
**April.** Comes down with acute attack of pneumonia.
**May.** Joins *Ashibi*, directed by Shūōshi.

1938 **September.** Publishes third book of haiku: *Summer Noon [Enchū]* (Sanseidō).

1940 First poem cut in stone erected at the Gōra Hotel, Hakone, Ashigara Shimo-gun, Kanagawa Prefecture.

1941 **September.** Moves to Tomida, Matsugaura, in Yokkaichi.

1942 **May.** Leaves the Sumitomo Main office. Changes conditions of employment to part-time.
**September.** Publishes fourth book of haiku: *Seven Days of the Week [Shichiyō]* (Sanseidō).

1945 **June.** Loses house in Saishōyama, in bombing raid.
**November.** Father, Shinsuke, dies.

1946 **June.** Moves to the Amagasuka coast, in Yokkaichi.
**July.** Publishes fifth book of haiku: *Fierce Waves [Gekirō]* (Seijisha).
**July.** Meets Saitō Sanki .

1947 **June.** Publishes sixth book of haiku: *Distant Star [Ensei].* (Sōgensha).
**December.** Publishes seventh book of haiku: *Evening [Bankoku]* (Sōgensha).

1948 **January.** *Sirius [Tenrō]* magazine begins publication (Yōtokusha). Publisher: Yamaguchi Seishi. Editor: Saitō Sanki. Editorial Board: Akimoto Fujio (aka Azuma Kyōzō), Hashimoto Takako, Hirahata Seitō, Takahashi Kenji, Yamaguchi Hatsujo, and six others.
**October.** Moves to Tsuzumi-ga-ura, in Shiroko-machi, Suzuka.

1949 **April.** Receives the Chūnichi Culture Award from the Chūbu Nippon Newspaper.

1950 **May.** Publishes eighth book of haiku: *Blue Goddess [Seijo]* (The Chūbu Nippon Newspaper).

1953 **September.** Suffers great damage to his home as a result of a typhoon.
**October.** Officiates in the ceremony of moving the Ise Shrine, which takes place every twenty years.

October. Moves his dwelling place to Kurakuen 5-banchō, in Nishinomiya.

1955    January. Publishes ninth book of haiku: *Japanese Clothes [Wafuku]*, (Kadokawa Shoten).

1956    November. Receives the Ōsaka Citizens Culture Award from the City of Ōsaka.

1957    April. Becomes Judge of the *Asahi Newspaper* Haiku Column.

1962    October. Younger sister, Ōta Saku, dies.

1967    February. Publishes tenth book of haiku: *Truss Bridge [Kōkyō]* (Shunjūsha). May. Publishes eleventh book of haiku: *Azimuth [Hōi]*, (Shunjūsha). August. Publishes twelfth book of haiku: *Bronze [Seidō]*, (Shunjūsha).

1970    February. Travels to Hong Kong, Bangkok, Angkor Wat, and Jakarta. From this time forth, will make foreign travel a yearly custom. November. Receives the Purple Ribbon Medal *[Shijuhōshō]*.

1973    October. Takes part again in the renewal ceremony of the Ise Shrine.

1976    May. Receives the Third Order of the Sacred Treasure *[Zuihōshō]*.

1977    January-October. Publishes ten-volume edition of *The Complete Works of Yamaguchi Seishi* (Meiji Shoin). March. Publishes thirteenth book of haiku: *One Corner [Ichigū]* (Shunjūsha). May. Publishes fourteenth book of haiku: *Unmoving [Fudō]* (Shunjūsha).

1979    June. Publishes *Selected Poems by Yamaguchi Seishi, with Notes by the Poet* (The Association of Haiku Poets).

1984    September. Publishes fifteenth book of haiku: *Snowy Peak [Setsugaku]* (Meiji Shoin). November. Younger sister, Shimoda Retsu, dies (pen name, Jikka).

1985    June. Wife, Hatsujo, dies.

1986    August. Receives the Blue Ribbon Medal *[Konjuhōshō]*. December. Establishes the Yamaguchi Seishi Fund for the Promotion of Science at Kōbe University.

1987    June. Receives the Japan Arts Academy Award. December. Shōnozaki Tatsue, younger sister and last of his three siblings, dies.

1988    July. Receives Honorary Doctorate from Kōbe University, becoming the first Japanese so honored by a Japanese National University. September. Celebration of *Tenrō*'s fortieth year in publication.

1989    January. Receives the *Asahi Newspaper* Award. October. *Tenrō* publishes its 500th issue.

1990    August. Travels to the Iguasu Falls, and elsewhere in Brazil.

**December.** Celebration of the beginning of his ninetieth year.

1991     **May.** Publication of sixteenth book of haiku, *Scarlet Sun [Kōjitsu]* (Meiji Shoin).

        **October.** Erection of 177th poem in stone (Chōon Temple, Aichi Prefecture).

1992     **November.** Recipient of the national Award for Cultural Merit.

*Nyorai dete te ni uketamō shidareume  (307)*

# Stone Monuments Bearing Seishi's Haiku

Since 1940, Seishi's fans have honored
him by having his poems engraved into
stone monuments placed throughout
Japan. By June of 1992 the monuments
numbered 181 in all.

    The highest is located on the
summit of Mount Fuji—the highest
point in Japan:

> *Standing at the top*
> *of the precipitous drop*
> *of Mount Fuji's wall. (255)*

The furthest north is on Sado Island,
and the furthest south is at Mabuni-ga-
oka, in Okinawa:

> *This burgeoning hill*
> *at the end of the island,*
> *the end of the world. (305)*

    The relationship of the homeland to its haiku is apt to be irrefutable in any
nation, and the number of haiku in this volume that have been particularly
selected for inscription at related places is significant—eighty-one. The
collection is thus particularly useful to readers traveling in Japan. The note
for each poem so honored has been clearly marked with a ✦ diamond.

学問の　　さびしさに堪へ　炭をつぐ

Gakumon no　　sabishisa ni tae　　sumi o tsugu

## *Bearing up under*
## *the loneliness of study,*
## *I add fresh charcoal.*

Composed 1924.
A boarding house in Hongō, in Tōkyō. I was studying law at Tōkyō
University. How confining, how lonely is the study of law. To get by,
I added charcoal and got warm.

---

✦  Season Word: *sumi* ,"charcoal." Winter, life.

*Vocabulary:*
- *sabishisa* is a noun form of the adjective *sabishii*, "lonely."
- 堪へ *tahe* is the traditional spelling of 堪え(る), *tae(ru),* "to bear with/endure."
  Even when spelled in the traditional manner, the word is pronounced without the
  *h* sound.

流氷や　宗谷の門波　荒れやまず
*Ryūhyō ya　Sōya no tonami　areyamazu*

# *Roughness unceasing —*
# *ice floes caught in clashing tides*
# *in the Sōya straits.*

Composed 1926.
Recalling Sakhalin. I was aboard ship, transferring from the Ōdomari Middle School to Kyōto Middle School #1. The waves were rough in the Sōya straits, and ice floes went by. The ship plowed her way through the floes.

---

Season Word: *ryūhyō,* "ice floes." Spring, topography.
　　　　　　Seishi originated this season word.

*Vocabulary:*
- *ya* in haiku is a *kireji*, or "cutting word," which generally has the effect of dividing the poem into two parts, as with a long dash or colon; in many cases it also gives the feeling of an exclamation.
- *tonami*, lit. "(sea)gate waves," has been a poetic word for the clashing waves/tides in narrow sea straits since the *Man'yōshū* (ca. 759).
- *are* is from *areru*, "become rough/rage/be wild," and *yamazu* is the classical negative form of *yamu*, "cease/end." Together they make a compound verb meaning "be rough/rage unceasingly."

*Other points of interest:*
- the young Seishi lived in Sakhalin with his grandfather from 1912 to 1917.

2

凍港や　　旧露の街は　　ありとのみ
*Tōkō ya*　　*kyū-Ro no machi wa*　　*ari to nomi*

# *A frozen harbor —*
## *what was once a Russian town*
## *there and nothing more.*

Composed 1926.
Recalling Sakhalin. While I was a middle school student, I went into
the old town of Ōdomari. Some Russians were still living there. The
harbor was frozen hard, suffusing the streets of the old Russian town
in silence.

---

Season Word: *tōkō,* "frozen harbor." Winter, season.

*Vocabulary:*
- *kyū-* is a prefix meaning "old/former/ex-" and 露 is an abbreviation of the kanji
  for "Russia," 露西亜, read *Roshia*.
- *machi* ("town"), when written 街 refers to the actual physical streets and districts
  of a town/city rather than to an administrative unit.
- *ari* is a classical form meaning "exists."
- *nomi* = "only/merely/barely."

*Other points of interest:*
- *Tōkō* became the title of Seishi's first book of poems, published in 1932. It asso-
  ciated the rising poet with the stark scenery of Japan's northern territory.

3

郭公や　韃靼の日の　沒るなべに

*Kakkō ya　　Dattan no hi no　　iru nabe ni*

# A cuckoo singing
# in the fading radiance
# of the Tartar sun.

Composed 1926.
Recalling the Sakhalin of my elementary school student years. I am in
the outskirts of Toyohara and can hear a cuckoo singing in the
primeval forest. As the sun moves westward over the Siberian
Maritime Province, his song goes on and on.

---

Season Word: *kakkō,* "cuckoo." Summer, animals.

*Vocabulary:*
- *Dattan* = "Tartar(s)," referring to various tribes that historically inhabited the area north of China on the Asian mainland. They are perhaps most easily thought of as descendants of Genghis Khan. *Dattan no hi* implies "sun (setting) over Tartary."
- *iru* ("enter into") is often written 沒る (or 没る) when referring to the sun dropping "into/beyond" the Western horizon.
- *nabe ni* following a verb means "accompanying/at the same time as/together with (the action)."

4

橇行や　　氷下魚の穴に　　海溢る
*Kyōkō ya*　　*komai no ana ni*　　*umi afuru*

# *Journeying by sleigh —*
# *a hole cut for ice fishing*
# *brimming with the sea.*

Composed 1927.
Recalling Sakhalin. People were fishing through holes in the ice in
Ōdomari, and I, a middle school student, went to watch. When a
sleigh went by, the ice buckled, and water brimmed from one of the
holes in the ice.

Season Word: *komai*, "fish commonly caught under ice." Winter, animals.

*Vocabulary:*
- *kyōkō* is written with kanji for "sleigh" (橇, by itself read *sori*) and "go" for a word meaning "going/traveling by sleigh." Though describing an action, it functions as a noun.
- strictly speaking, *komai* is the name for a kind of cod, but since it's written with kanji meaning "ice" + "under" + "fish," it can be thought of as a generic name for any fish that is fished through holes in the ice.
- *afuru* is the classical form of modern *afureru*, "overflow/brim over/flood." The last line is equivalent to *umi ga afureru* in modern Japanese, "the sea brims over."

5

匙 なめて　童 たのしも　夏氷
*Saji namete*　*warabe tanoshi mo*　*natsugōri*

# *The rapture of it —*
# *little boy licking the spoon*
# *that held summer ice.*

Composed 1927.
A boy eats shaved ice with sugar syrup from a bowl. Scooping the ice
water with a spoon of thin aluminum, he sips, licks the spoon, and
tastes the chill. It was long ago. We don't have such spoons now.

---

Season Word: *natsugōri* ,"summer ice." Summer, life.

*Vocabulary:*
- *warabe* means "child," but in general use the presumption tends to be that it re-
fers to a boy.
- *tanoshi* has become *tanoshii* ("[is] pleasant/happy/cheerful/enjoyable") in mod-
ern Japanese. *Warabe (wa) tanoshi* means "the child is happy/the child is enjoy-
ing himself."
- *natsugōri*, literally "summer ice," refers to a summer treat still popular today
called *kōrimizu*. A tall mound of shaved ice in a bowl is topped with brightly col-
ored sugar syrup and eaten with a spoon.

日蔽や　キネマの衢　鬱然と
*Hiōi ya　kinema no chimata　utsuzen-to*

# *A row of awnings —*
# *darkness settles down upon*
# *the movie district.*

Composed 1927.

Dōtonbori, the movie district of Ōsaka. The street was dark under a row of awnings. It was like the darkness under a deep sea. I had graduated from the university and was working for Sumitomo and living in the company dormitory in Unagidani. I often visited Dōtonbori.

---

Season Word: *hiōi*, "awnings." Summer, life.

*Vocabulary:*
- *ya* is a *kireji* ("cutting word") dividing the poem into two parts, and giving the feeling of an exclamation.
- *utsuzen-to* is an adverb that can mean either "gloomily/cheerlessly" or "in a lively/flourishing/energetic manner." While describing how dark the street seems under the awnings, it also suggests the possibility of a street crowded with movie-goers.

*Other points of interest:*
- Dōtonbori has been a famous entertainment district since the Tokugawa era (1600–1867), stretching for a mile and a half through central Ōsaka along the southern bank of the Dōtonbori Canal.

7

# 七月の　　青嶺まぢかく　熔鉱炉

*Shichigatsu no　　aone majikaku　　yōkōro*

## *Smelting furnaces,*
## *flush up against high mountains*
## *verdant with July.*

Composed 1927.
On a business trip to Kyūshū, I visited the Yawata Iron and Steel
plant. I looked at the hot smelting furnaces, then went outside and
saw the green mountains in front of me. It was midsummer. How
beautiful are high green mountains in July!

---

✦  Season Word: *shichigatsu*, "July." Summer, season.

*Vocabulary:*
- *majikaku* is the adverb form of *majikai* ("be close at hand/very near"), from *ma* ("space") and *chikai* ("close/near"; *ch* changes to *j* for euphony). Use of the adverb form implies a verb like *aru* ("exists") or *mieru* ("can be seen").

*Other points of interest:*
- Yawata Iron and Steel Works, in modern-day Kita-Kyūshū city, has been Japan's largest steel mill since it was established by the government in 1901. The massive mill was apparently producing about half of Japan's steel around the time Seishi visited it in 1927.

8

# 釘 うてる　天主の手足　露の花圃

*Kugi uteru*　　*tenshu no teashi*　　*tsuyu no kaho*

## *The Lord's hands and feet,*
## *with the nails hammered through them —*
## *dewdrops on blossoms.*

Composed 1927.
On a business trip to Nagasaki, in Kyūshū, I visited the Ōura Catholic
Church and the image of Jesus on the cross in the flower garden. Nails
in his hands and feet. Dewdrops on the flowers in the garden. I thought
of the blood flowing on his hands and feet.

---

Season Word: *tsuyu*, "dew." Autumn, celestial phenomena.

*Vocabulary:*
- *uteru* is classical Japanese for *utte aru*, "have been nailed," from *utsu* (lit. "strike/hit," but
  with nails, "pound/drive/nail") and *aru* ("exists").
- *tenshu*, combining kanji for "heaven" and "master," is one of the words used to refer to the
  Christian God originally introduced to Japan by Catholic missionaries in the sixteenth cen-
  tury. Today the word has an archaic flavor.
- *kaho* refers to a whole garden of flowers, not merely a few blossoms.

*Other points of interest:*
- Nagasaki was one of the principal areas of missionary activity when Christianity was intro-
  duced to Japan in the sixteenth century. Ōura Catholic Church was built in 1864 and dedi-
  cated to 26 Christians crucified in 1597. Today the church has been designated a national
  treasure.

かの巫女の　　手焙の手を　　恋ひわたる
*Kano miko no*　　*teaburi no te o*　　*koi wataru*

## *The shrine maiden's hands held over the charcoal pan radiated love.*

Composed 1928.
I often visited Nara. Once when I visited Wakamiya, in Kasuga, I saw a shrine maiden on the cold Kagura stage holding her hands over a brazier. The charcoal fire was beautifully reflected in her soft hands. I remember her hands.

---

Season Word: *teaburi*, "charcoal pan." Winter, life.

*Vocabulary:*
- *miko* formerly meant "shaman," referring to women who could communicate with the Shinto *kami* ("gods/powers"); today *miko* can refer to any woman who plays a ceremonial role at a Shinto shrine.
- 恋ひ, spelled *kohi* but read *koi*, refers to romantic love/yearnings, or simply to a strong attraction to something. *Hi* in the old spelling can also mean "fire," suggesting "flames of passion" as an image associated with romantic love. Here, *hi wataru* ("fire crosses") implies that the glowing coals reflect across the *miko*'s hands, while use of the word *koi* suggests how strongly the poet was attracted to the figure of this maiden warming her hands.

*Other points of interest:*
- Wakamiya is a subshrine of the large Kasuga Shrine (founded: 709) in Nara, one of the most important shrines in Japanese history.

落ち羽子に　潮の穂さきの　走りて来

*Ochi hago ni*　　*shio no hosaki no*　　*hashirite ku*

# *Shuttlecock falling*
## *where the surf comes crashing in,*
## *running toward it.*

Composed 1928.
We were playing battledore and shuttlecock on the beach, and when a
shuttlecock fell on the beach, the spume of the surf came running
directly toward it. The forefront of the waves was about to engulf it.

---

Season Word: *hago*, "shuttlecock." New Year's, life.

*Vocabulary:*
- *shio*, when written 潮, refers to the tide or seawater.
- *hosaki* can be the whitecapped crest of a wave, but here it refers to the foamy edge of the surf as it advances up the beach.
- *hashirite* is the old *-te* form of *hashiru* ("run").
- *ku* is the dictionary form of *kuru* ("come") in classical Japanese; as in modern Japanese, this form doubles as the plain/abrupt form for ending sentences. *Hashirite ku* = "comes running."

*Other points of interest:*
- the Japanese battledore is a long, rectangular wooden paddle, and the shuttlecock is a tiny wooden ball with feathers attached.

11

手花火に　　妹がかひなの　　照さるる
*Tehanabi ni*　　*imo ga kaina no*　　*terasaruru*

## *My beloved's arm,*
### *above the sparkler she holds,*
### *shining in the gloom.*

Composed 1928.
During my engagement. I was visiting my fiancée at her home. When
a magnesium sparkler held by her was ignited, bright fire lighted up
her arm. A girl's arm illuminated by a sparkler!

---

Season Word: *tehanabi*, "sparkler." Summer, life.

*Vocabulary:*
- *imo* 妹 is written with the kanji used for the modern word *imōto*, "younger sister,"
  but in classical/poetic Japanese it refers to the man's beloved/betrothed/wife.
- *ga* is like the possessive *no* in modern Japanese.
- かひな is the traditional spelling of かいな *kaina*, which strictly speaking refers
  to the upper arm but is sometimes used for the arm as a whole. Taken together,
  *imo ga kaina* is like modern *koibito/fianse no ude*, "my lover's/fiancée's arm."
- *no* marks the subject, like modern *ga* (in modifying clauses, *no* can still replace
  *ga* today).
- *terasaruru* is an old passive form of *terasu* ("shine light on/illumine").

12

はたはたは　　わぎもが肩を　　越えゆけり
Hatahata wa        wagimo ga kata o        koe yukeri

# *Flying grasshopper*
# *passing over the shoulder*
# *of my lady love.*

Composed 1928.
We went to Unzen on our honeymoon, and as we walked on the
summit road, a grasshopper flew from behind us, passing over my
new wife's shoulder. Fate made the grasshopper fly over us.

---

Season Word: *hatahata*, "flying grasshopper." Autumn, animals.

*Vocabulary:*
- *wagimo* is a contraction of *wa ga imo*, where *wa* = "I/me," *ga* is possessive, and *imo* = "beloved/betrothed" → "my beloved." The *ga* that follows is also possessive.
- *koe* is the stem of *koeru* ("go/pass over") and *yukeri* is a form of *iku* ("go") equivalent to the modern plain/abrupt past form, *itta*. Following another verb, *iku/itta* indicates that the action moves/moved away from the speaker.

扇風器　大き翼を　やすめたり
*Senpūki　ōki tsubasa o　yasumetari*

**Fan on the ceiling
slowing, coming to a stop,
resting its great wings.**

Composed 1929.
The ceiling fan in my office at Sumitomo had four wings, forming a cross. When it was turning, the wings were invisible, but when its speed slowed, they took shape. When the fan stopped we could see the four wings in a cross.

---

Season Word: *senpūki*, "(electric) fan." Summer, life.

*Vocabulary:*
- *ōki* is a contraction of *ōkii/ōki-na* ("large").
- *yasumetari* is a classical equivalent of *yasumete-iru* ("is resting [something]"), from *yasumeru* ("to rest [something]").
- more literally the Japanese says: Fan/its great wings/resting.

雌の熊の　　皮やさしけれ　　雄とあれば
*Me no kuma no*　　*kawa yasashikere*　　*o to areba*

*How soft is the nap*
*of a female bear's skin*
*when a male's is near.*

Composed 1930.
In the parlor of my wife's parents' house, two bearskins were spread
each winter. One was a male bear's skin; the other was a female's.
They were different in size, and had different nap, too. One was hard;
the other was soft. The softness of the female when next to a male.

Season Word: *kuma*, "bear." Winter, animals.

*Vocabulary:*
- *yasashikere* is a classical exclamatory form of *yasashii* ("gentle/tender/soft").
- *to* = "with"
- *areba* is from the classical verb *ari* ("be/exist"), equivalent to modern *aru*. This
  *-ba* form means "when/because" ( . . . *to areba* = "when/because is with . . ."); 
  "if" would be *araba*.
- the poem is in inverted syntax; in normal syntax, *o to areba* would come first.

15

青海の　めらめらと燃ゆ　走馬燈
Ao-umi　no　meramera-to moyu　sōmatō

# *Revolving lantern*
## *touching off its own blue sea*
### *in a crackling blaze.*

Composed 1931.
A revolving lantern I bought from a night stall at the Sankō shrine, in
my town. The candle must have fallen, because the lantern began to
burn. The blue sea drawn on the lantern was enveloped in scarlet
flames. It was odd to see the blue sea catch fire.

---

Season Word: *sōmatō*, "revolving lantern." Summer, life.

*Vocabulary:*
- *meramera* is a word that represents the effect of flames, usually quite intense flames. Adding *-to* essentially makes it an adverb modifying *moyu*, the classical form of *moeru* ("burn/blaze").
- *no* marks *ao-umi* ("blue sea") as the subject of *moyu*.
- strictly speaking, *moyu* cannot modify *sōmatō*, so it is as if *aoumi no meramera-to moyu* ("the blue sea burns *meramera*") is followed by a colon.
- *sōmato* is literally "running horse lantern" → "revolving lantern." It is a paper device, part of which is made to revolve by the heat of a candle. The revolving element is usually brightly painted — sometimes with horses or people; here with a sea illustration.

16

かりかりと　　蟷螂蜂の　　皃を食む
*Karikari to*　　*tōrō hachi no*　　*kao o hamu*

## *A praying mantis*
## *chomping noisily upon*
## *the face of a bee.*

Composed 1932.
I saw a praying mantis in the compound of the Shijōnawate shrine. It
had caught a bee and was beginning to eat it. The praying mantis,
with its strong teeth, was chewing noisily on the bee's face.

---

Season Word: *tōrō*, "praying mantis." Autumn, animals.

*Vocabulary:*
- *karikari* represents the effect of crispness/crunchiness. Adding *-to* makes it an
  adverb modifying *hamu* ("eat/feed on").
- *tōrō* = "praying mantis" and *hachi* = "bee"; for rhythmic reasons, the particle *wa*
  (or *ga*) has been omitted between the two words.

スケートの　　紐むすぶ間も　　逸りつつ
*Sukēto no*　　*himo musubu ma mo*　　*hayari tsutsu*

***Even in the time***
***it takes to tie on ice-skates,***
***the heart beats faster.***

Composed 1932.
The skating rink on the top of the Asahi Building, near the Sumitomo Building. Since I had become expert at skating with *geta* skates when I was in elementary school, I was able to master the use of shoeskates quickly. My heart would pound even as I tied the laces of my skates.

---

Season Word: *sukēto*, "ice skates." Winter, life.

*Vocabulary:*
- *sukēto no himo musubu* is a complete thought/sentence ("[I] tie the laces of [my] skates") modifying *ma*.
- *ma* means "gap/span/space between," here referring to a span of time.
- *hayari* is from *hayaru* ("be rash/impatient"), and in this context *tsutsu* carries both of its common meanings — that something is continuing/progressing and that two things are occurring at the same time.

*Other points of interest:*
- the so-called *geta*-skate had a single blade in place of the two usual "teeth" under the *geta*, and slipped onto the feet like thongs.

18

薔薇垣の　夜は星のみぞ　かがやける

Baragaki no　yo wa hoshi nomi zo　kagayakeru

*Over the rose hedge,*
*night has settled; nothing shines*
*except for the stars.*

Composed 1932.
From my home in Tamatsukuri, I commuted to my office in the
Sumitomo Building, in Tosabori. The streetcar ran below the red rose
hedge of the Shimizudani Girl's High School. When our streetcar
passed there at night after work, the hedge was invisible. We could
see nothing but twinkling stars.

Season Word: *bara*, "rose." Summer, plants.

*Vocabulary:*
- *no* is the modern attributive/possessive *no*, so *baragaki no yo* is literally "the rose hedge's night/the night of the rose hedge" → "the rose hedge at night."
- emphatic *zo* in classical/poetic language has none of the "rough" feeling of modern colloquial *zo*. Here the emphasis is on *nomi* ("only"): "only (the stars) and nothing else."
- *kagayakeru* is a classical form of *kagayaku* ("shine/glisten/gleam/twinkle").

*Other points of interest:*
- references to Sumitomo in the author's notes indicate that the other places mentioned are also in Ōsaka.

19

男の雛も　　まなこかぼそく　　波の間に
*O no hina mo*　　*manako kabosoku*　　*nami no ma ni*

# *Even the male doll*
## *holds his eyes in narrow slits*
### *tossing on the waves.*

Composed 1933.
I visited the storehouse of ancient dolls at Awashima shrine, in Kata, in Wakayama. I thought of the ceremony of floating dolls out on the sea. The eyes of the old dolls, even the male doll, were narrow. The male doll would float away on the waves along with the female doll, both with their eyes in narrow slits.

---

Season Word: *hina,* "festival doll." Spring, observances.

*Vocabulary:*
- *manako* originally referred to the dark portion (pupil and iris) of the eye but is often used to mean the entire eye.
- *kabosoku* is the adverb form of *kabosoi* ("slender/fragile/feeble"), from the intensifying prefix *ka-* and *hosoi* ("thin/narrow"; *h* changes to *b* for euphony).

祭あはれ　覘きの眼鏡　曇るさへ
*Matsuri aware　nozoki no megane　kumoru sae*

# *Festival pathos —*
# *when even the peep-show scopes*
# *are besmeared with fog.*

Composed 1933.
They had a peep show device at the summer festival. A scene of a
drama could be seen, magnified through a convex lens. When I
looked through, the lens was fogged over. Boys had clouded the lens
by bringing their faces too close. Festival pathos!

---

Season Word: *matsuri*, "festival." Summer, observances.

*Vocabulary:*
- *aware* most basically refers to "depth of feeling/deep feelings." In modern use this is more often "sorrow/grief/sympathy/pity," but it can also be "wonder/charm/tenderness/compassion" → "pathos." In classical Japanese, reading the kana character は as *wa* was not reserved only for when it was a particle.
- *nozoki* is the noun form of *nozoku* ("peep/look into").
- さへ, read *sae*, is an emphatic "even –."

祭 あはれ　奇術をとめを　恋ひ焦れ
*Matsuri aware*　*kijutsu otome o*　*koi kogare*

## *Festival pathos:*
## *falling hopelessly in love*
## *with a lady juggler.*

Composed 1933.
I saw a magic show at a summer festival booth when I was a boy.
There was a lady juggler with thick makeup, dressed in foreign style.
She seemed to a boy the fairest of the fair. I fell madly in love with
her. Again, festival pathos!

---

Season Word: *matsuri*, "festival." Summer, observances.

*Vocabulary:*
- 奇 *ki* means "unusual/strange/mysterious" and 術 *jutsu* refers to a trick or an act that requires special skill, so the combination means "conjuring tricks/magic/ jugglery."
- をとめ is the traditional spelling for おとめ *otome*, ("virgin/maiden/girl"). In classical Japanese, を was not reserved only for use as a particle.
- *kogare* is from *kogareru* ("yearn for/pine for/be hungry for"), and is often used in combination with *koi* (see poem 10) as a kind of intensifier.

夏草に　　汽罐車の車輪　　来て止る
*Natsukusa ni*　　*kikansha no sharin*　　*kite tomaru*

*Up to summer grass,*
*wheels of a locomotive*
*coming to a stop.*

Composed 1933.
A station yard thick with summer grass. A locomotive comes in and
stops there. It brings its wheels to a halt and stops. Summer grass
juxtaposed with train wheels.

---

Season Word: *natsukusa*, "summer grass." Summer, plants.

*Vocabulary:*
- *ga*, to mark the subject, has been omitted after *sharin* ("wheels") for rhythmic purposes.
- *kite* is the *-te* form of *kuru* ("come"), so *kite tomaru* is literally like "comes and stops."

蟋蟀を　　あはれと放つ　　掌を見たり
*Hatahata o*　　　*aware to hanatsu*　　　*te o mitari*

# *Looking at a hand*
## *as it thoughtfully sets free*
## *a trapped grasshopper.*

Composed 1933.
A young woman enjoying herself in a field had caught a grasshopper,
which she set free, saying, "Poor thing!" I looked at her hand. (She
was a student of mine in the Sumitomo Training School for Nurses).

---

Season Word: *hatahata*, "grasshopper." Autumn, animals.

*Vocabulary:*
- *aware to hanatsu* is short for something like *aware to omotte hanatsu*, "feels pity/sympathy and releases."
- *te* means "hand" but the kanji 掌, normally read *tanagokoro* or *tenohira*, refers specifically to the palm of the hand.
- *mitari* can be the equivalent of either *mita* ("watched/looked at/saw") or *mite-iru* ("is watching/looking at") in modern Japanese.

24

東風 の 波　　埠頭 の 鉄鎖　　濡れそぼつ
*Kochi no nami*　　*futō no tessa*　　*nure sobotsu*

*Driven by east winds,*
*　　combers drench the pier chains*
*　　under wild water.*

Composed 1934.
I went out on a pier at Ōsaka Harbor. Waves driven by east winds
splashed against the pier, sending up a cloud of spray and dousing the
pier chains. Chains go with piers, especially wet chains.

---

Season Word: *kochi*, "east wind." Spring, celestial phenomena.

*Vocabulary:*
- *kochi* is one of quite a few words describing specific kinds of wind in Japanese, in
  this case "east wind." The kanji 東風 mean "east" and "wind," respectively, and
  can also be read *higashikaze*.
- both *nure(ru)* and *sobotsu* mean "become wet," but *sobotsu* implies "soaked/
  sopping wet."

葭原に　　真の雀の　　ゐてなきつ

*Yoshihara ni    shin no suzume no    ite nakitsu*

# In the pampas grass,
# I find a real sparrow,
# sitting and singing.

Composed 1934.

In the pampas-grass field [*yoshihara*], a *yoshihara* sparrow was singing: "Gyo-gyoshi, gyo-gyoshi." I also heard a "Chun, chun" in the pampas grass, but it was not a yoshihara sparrow. Instead it was an ordinary sparrow. A real one!

---

Season Word: *suzume*, "sparrow." Summer, animals.

*Vocabulary:*
- *yoshihara* is literally "pampas-grass field."
- the *no* following *suzume* ("sparrow") marks it as the subject of *ite nakitsu*.
- ゐ is a kana character that is no longer used. It belonged to the *wa*-column of the kana chart, and was once pronounced *wi*, but it has long been pronounced *i*.
- *ite* is the *-te* form of *iru*, which originally meant "to be sitting" but eventually came to mean "be/exist" for animate things.
- *nakitsu* is a classical equivalent of *naita*, the past form of *naku* ("[a bird] sings/ chirps").

26

玄海の　冬浪を大と　見て寝ねき

*Genkai no　fuyunami o dai to　mite ineki*

## *Watching the great waves*
## *in Genkai's wintry sea road;*
## *then going to sleep.*

Composed 1934.
I was on a business trip to Manchuria. Our steamer left Shimonoseki and started into the Genkai Sea. Overcome by the great waves in that winter sea, I went into my cabin and lay down. The word "Great" is eerie.

---

Season Word: *fuyunami*, "wintry waves." Winter, topography.

*Vocabulary:*
- *fuyunami o dai to mi(ru)* literally means "see the winter waves as great," but suggests also that he saw the waves as "looking like the [sweeping curves of the] kanji 大." In the original author note, it is this kanji that is called "eerie."
- *ineki* is a classical equivalent of *neta*, the past form of *neru* ("lie down/go to sleep").

# 緯度 高く 船の煖房 通ひそむ

*Ido takaku      fune no danbō      kayoisomu*

## *Ship's heating system*
## *coming on with the movement*
## *to high latitude.*

Composed 1934.
On our way north to Dairen by steamer, we moved gradually higher
in latitude. I was made aware of it by the sound of steam passing
through the heat pipes in the cabin.

---

Season Word: *danbō*, "heating system." Winter, life.

*Vocabulary:*
- *takaku* is the adverb form of *takai* ("high"), and implies something like *takaku naru*, "become higher/rise."
- 通ひ is the traditional spelling of *kayoi*, from *kayou* ("come and go/circulate").
- *-somu* is the old form of *-someru*, a verb suffix meaning "begin/start to."

# ただ見る　起き伏し枯野の　起き伏し
### Tada miru　　okifushi kareno no　　okifushi

## *All that meets the eye:*
## *brown plains rising and falling,*
## *rising and falling.*

Composed 1934.
When I looked out on the withered fields from the top of the 203-meter Hill, in Port Arthur, I saw how the fields rose and fell. Soon afterward, I intoned to myself: "All that meets the eye: brown plains rising and falling, rising and falling." Broken meter.

---

Season Word: *kareno*, "field of withered grass." Winter, topography.

*Vocabulary:*
- *tada* = "just/only," so *tada miru* is literally "[I] just look."
- *oki* is from *okiru* ("rise/get up") and *fushi* is the noun form of *fusu* ("lie down"). Normally, *okifushi* means "waking and sleeping" — i.e., going about one's life — and it is another word formed with the same kanji, 起伏 *kifuku*, that refers to the "undulations/rising and falling/hilliness" of terrain.

*Other points of interest:*
- Port Arthur fell into Japanese hands after a long and bloody seige in the Russo-Japanese War. The 203 Meter Hill, which commands the harbor of the city, was captured by Japanese over six months before the city fell.

枯野 来て　帝王の階を　わが登る

*Kareno kite　　teiō no kai o　　waga noboru*

## *I cross a dry field*
## *and then walk up a staircase*
## *where Emperors trod.*

Composed 1934.

The North Mausoleum, in Mukden, was in a withered field. I passed through the gate and found a staircase in front of me. It was a staircase up which Emperors ascended. I walked up the stairs and approached the mausoleum filled with awe. I trod the "Emperor's staircase."

---

Season Word: *kareno*, "field of withered grass." Winter, topography.

*Vocabulary:*
- *o* has been omitted after *kareno* ("withered/dry field"). The phrase – *o kite* (from *kuru*, "come") means "coming through/along/across."
- *waga* = "I/me."

陵さむく　　日月空に　　照らしあふ

*Ryō samuku　jitsugetsu sora ni　terashiau*

# *Over the cold tomb,*
# *sun and moon in the heavens*
# *shine at each other.*

Composed 1934.

It was cold at the North Mausoleum. I looked up and saw the sun and moon riding high in the sky. They were bright and shone facing each other. The sky of the mausoleum was decorated with the luminous bodies of the sun and the moon.

---

Season Word: *samuku*, "cold." Winter, season.

*Vocabulary:*
- *samuku* is a continuing form of the adjective *samui* ("cold"), implying "is cold, and . . ."
- *jitsugetsu* is a "poetic" word for "sun and moon."
- *terashi* is from *terasu* ("illuminate/cast light on"), and *-au* (あふ is the old spelling of あう) is a verb suffix indicating that the action is somehow "mutual/being exchanged" → "illumine/shine at each other."

掌に　　枯野の低き　日を愛づる
*Tenohira ni　kareno no hikuki　hi o mezuru*

# *The palm of one hand*
# *caresses the sun setting*
# *over withered fields.*

Composed 1934.

I left for Sinkiang on the Limited Express Asia, across a boundless expanse of withered fields. The sun was on its way down, hanging low in the west. I placed the sun on the palm of my hand and thought: "This is the Manchurian sun."

---

Season Word: *kareno*, "field of withered grass." Winter, topography.

*Vocabulary:*
- *hikuki* is the classical equivalent of modern *hikui* ("low"), but is the form used only for directly modifying a noun. *Hikuki hi* = "the low sun" → "the falling/sinking sun" (never "the rising sun").
- *mezuru* is the classical equivalent of *mederu*, which basically means "enjoy/admire/be attracted to [something]," and in common use can mean both "to love" and "to praise." A palm shows love/praise in "caresses."

# 氷る河　わたる車室の　裡白む
### Kōru kawa　wataru shashitsu no　uchi shiramu

## *Coach interior*
## *whitens as the train crosses*
## *a frozen river.*

Composed 1934.
The Sung Hua River was frozen over. My train crossed it by an iron bridge. The light reflected off the ice sheet brightened the inside of the coach with a whiteness that made me feel cold.

---

Season Word: *kōru*, "to freeze." Winter, topography.

*Vocabulary:*
- *kōru kawa* can be thought of either as set off by a colon, or as part of the complete thought/sentence *kōru kawa (o) wataru* ("cross the freezing river"), which modifyies *shashitsu* (lit. "[train]car room" → "coach interior").
- *no* turns *shashitsu* into a modifier for *uchi*, which is a noun meaning "the inside": *shashitsu no uchi* = "the inside of the coach" → *(kōru kawa) wataru shashitsu no uchi* = "the inside of the coach crossing (the freezing river)."
- in normal syntax, *uchi* ("inside") would be followed by *ga*, marking it as the subject of *shiramu* ("grow white/bright"): "the inside . . . whitens/brightens."

氷る河　　見ればいよいよ　　しづかなり

*Kōru kawa*　　*mireba iyo-iyo*　　*shizuka nari*

### *The more I look at*
### *the river under ice pack,*
### *the calmer it grows.*

Composed 1934.

In Harbin, I stood by the Sung Hua River and gazed at its frozen surface. It was calm. The more I looked at it, the calmer it grew. It was the calm of frigidity.

---

Season Word: *kōru*, "to freeze." Winter, topography.

*Vocabulary:*
- *mireba* is the classical "when/because" form of *miru* ("see/look").
- *iyo-iyo* = "more and more/more than ever"
- *shizuka nari* is the classical equivalent of *shizuka da*, "is quiet/calm/tranquil." しづか is the old spelling of the word.

枯れし野に　　機翼を拡げ　　車輪を垂れ

*Kareshi no ni*　　*kiyoku o hiroge*　　*sharin o tare*

## *Over withered fields,*
## *the plane stretches out its wings*
## *and hangs down its wheels.*

Composed 1934.
I traveled by air from Harbin to Sinkiang. I had never flown in a
small plane before and looked about in fascination. Over brown
fields, the plane extended its wings and hung down its wheels in
complete safety.

---

Season Word: *kareshi no*, "field of withered grass." Winter, topography.

*Vocabulary:*
- *kareshi* is a classical equivalent of *kareta*, the past form of *kareru* ("wither"); it
  directly modifies *no* ("field[s]").
- 機 *ki*, in *kiyoku*, means "machine," and here stands for *hikōki* (lit. "flying ma-
  chine" → "airplane"), so *kiyoku* = "airplane wings."
- *hiroge* acts like the *-te* form of *hirogeru* ("spread"), meaning "spreads [its wings],
  and . . ."
- *tare* in classical Japanese is equivalent to both *tareru* ("dangle/hang down") and
  *tarasu* ("let dangle/let hang down") in modern language. Here it implies
  *tarashite-iru* ("[the plane] is letting [the wheels] hang down").

35

蜥蜴出て　新しき家の　主を眄たり
*Tokage dete*　　*atarashiki ie no*　　*shu o mitari*

*A lizard comes out
to observe the new owner
of this dwelling place.*

Composed 1935.
On my return from Manchuria, I came down with pneumonia, and recuperated in Ashiya. As I looked at the garden from the veranda, a lizard came out and gave me a sidelong glance. It was a look that seemed to say: "So this is the new owner of the house."

---

Season Word: *tokage*, "lizard." Summer, animals.

*Vocabulary:*
- *atarashiki* = modern *atarashii* ("new"); in classical Japanese the *-ki* form of the adjective is used for directly modifying nouns. *Atarashiki ie* = "new house" and *atarashiki ie no shu* = "new master of the house."
- *mitari* is a classical equivalent of *mita*, the past form of *miru* ("look/see"), but when written with the kanji 眄 it implies "give a sidewise glance/look askance."

するすると　岩をするすると　地を蜥蜴
*Surusuru-to*　　*iwa o surusuru-to*　　*chi o tokage*

*Gliding over rocks,*
*    gliding over open ground,*
*        lizard slipping by.*

Composed 1935.
The lizard glided over rocks, then got off the rocks and glided over
the ground. The "gliding over rocks" and "gliding over open ground"
are tied into one. This haiku, too, departs from the prescribed form.

Season Word: *tokage*, "lizard." Summer, animals.

*Vocabulary:*
- *surusuru* represents a slippery/sliding/gliding effect, and *-to* makes it an adverb
  meaning "in a slippery/sliding/gliding" manner. The implied verb at the end of
  the poem is something like *iku* ("go") or *hashiru* ("run"): *surusuru-to . . . tokage*
  *(ga iku)* = "the lizard glides."
- when *o* is followed by a motion verb like "go/come/walk/run," it marks the place
  where the motion goes "along/through/across" (see poem 30).

37

ピストルが　プールの硬き　面にひびき

*Pisutoru ga*　　*pūru no kataki*　　*mo ni hibiki*

# The sound of the gun
# rebounding from the surface
# of hard pool water.

Composed 1936.
A swimming meet. The swimmers awaited the report of the starting
gun. Then the gun went off. The sound that bounced off the hard
surface of the water was a hard sound.

---

Season Word: *pūru*, "swimming pool." Summer, life.

*Vocabulary:*
- *pisutoru*, from English "pistol," implies *pisutoru no oto*, "the sound of the pistol/gun."
- *kataki* is the classical *-ki* form of the adjective *katai* ("hard/rigid"), for directly modifying nouns.
- *mo* is an archaic word for *omote* ("surface").
- *hibiki* is a form of the verb *hibiku* ("to sound/echo/reverberate").

夏の河　　赤き鉄鎖の　　はし浸る
*Natsu no kawa　　akaki tessa no　　hashi hitaru*

## *The summer river*
## *immersing the scarlet end*
## *of an iron chain.*

Composed 1937.

We went down the Aji River in Ōsaka on a cruise and passed a chain factory. A long red chain was stretched out along the ground, its end dangling into the river. It was made to hold an anchor.

---

Season Word: *natsu no kawa*, "summer river." Summer, topography.

*Vocabulary:*
- *akaki* is the classical *-ki* form of modern *akai* ("red").
- *tessa* is literally "iron chain."

雪しろき　高嶺はあれど　阿蘇に侍す
*Yuki shiroki*　*takane wa aredo*　*Aso ni jisu*

## *Higher though they be,*
## *still those mountains under snow*
## *look up to Aso.*

Composed 1938.
As I made my way down Mount Aso, I turned and looked at the snowless mountain. Some of the mountains around it had snow on them and seemed higher, but they do not have the stature of Aso.

---

Season Word: *yuki*, "snow." Winter, celestial phenomena.

*Vocabulary:*
- *shiroki* is the classical *-ki* form of *shiroi* ("white").
- *aredo* is the "although" form of the classical verb *ari* ("be/exist").
- *jisu* is the classical form of *jisuru* ("attend/wait upon/be in service to").

*Other points of interest:*
- Mount Aso is the site of one of the largest volcanic calderas in the world. Included in it are five peaks, one of which is still blowing ash. Its shrine, Aso Jinja, has high status in Imperial circles. For almost 1,000 years, every Emperor has been expected to make an offering there at least once in his reign.

愛憐し児が　毛糸の襯衣を　手首にす

*Kanashi ko ga*　　*keito no shatsu o*　　*tekubi ni su*

### A *fetching baby*
### *swaddled in a woolen shirt,*
### *only hands showing.*

Composed 1938.
A baby is being dressed in a woolen shirt. The sleeves even cover his
wrists. A baby with sleeves over his wrists. A fetching baby.

---

Season Word: *keito*, "woolens." Winter, life.

*Vocabulary:*
- *kanashi* in classical Japanese can mean "dear/endearing/fetching" instead of
  "sad/sorrowful." Using the kanji 愛 ("love") and 憐 ("compassion/pity") makes
  the intended meaning clear.
- *su* is the classical form of *suru* ("do"); . . .*ni su/suru* can mean "put on/attach to/
  wear" when speaking of clothing and other things to wear.

41

火口湖が　白き氷盤と　なれるのみ
*Kakōko ga　shiroki hyōban to　nareru nomi*

# *Crater lake in ice —*
# *just an alabaster sheet*
# *over the crater.*

Composed 1939.
I was climbing Mount Karakuni, in Kagoshima Prefecture. As I climbed up a snow-covered road, I could see the crater lake below me was frozen. The crater lake had become a sheet of ice. A sheet of ice covering a lake formed by a crater!

---

Season Word: *hyōban*, "ice sheet." Winter, topography.

*Vocabulary:*
- *kakō*, literally "fire mouth," refers only to the crater of a volcano. The volcano as a whole is called 火山 *kazan*.
- *nareru* is a classical equivalent of *natta*, the past form of *naru* ("become"), and *nomi* = "just/only," so *(shiroki hyōban) to nareru nomi* literally means "became/ has become just (a white sheet of ice)."

# ひとの子の　頭巾なほして　天守の上

*Hito no ko no*　　　*zukin naoshite*　　　*tenshu no ue*

## *In a lord's sanctum,*
## *I adjust the winter hood*
## *on someone's baby.*

Composed 1939.

I had made my way up into the keep of Hakutei Castle, in Inuyama, from which I could see Mount Haku, off to the west. There was a baby on his mother's back, wearing a hood that almost covered his eyes. When I adjusted it, he was pleased at seeing the light.

---

Season Word: *zukin*, "winter hood." Winter, life.

*Vocabulary:*
- *hito* in this case means "stranger/somebody I don't know."
- なほして is the old spelling of なおして *naoshite*, the *-te* form of *naosu* ("fix/set right").

*Other points of interest:*
- one need not be a lover of Kurosawa films to be familiar with the great white tower with graceful rooflines that stands at the center of the sprawling grounds of a traditional Japanese castle. The keep at the top, or *tenshu*, was a lookout, command center, and final bastion in times of war, and a symbol/expression of the lord's power in times of peace.

ひとり膝を　抱けば秋風　また秋風
Hitori hiza o　dakeba akikaze　mata akikaze

*Huddled up alone*
*against the winds of autumn —*
*the winds of autumn.*

Composed 1940.
Something had happened to make me sad, and I sat alone, hugging
my knees. An autumn wind sprang up and passed over me. Then it
came again. Through it all, I bore my sadness.

---

Season Word: *akikaze*, "autumn wind." Autumn, celestial phenomena.

*Vocabulary:*
- *dakeba* is from *daku* ("hold in arms/hug/embrace"). The *-ba* form in this case
  means "when," not "if" or "because."
- *mata* = "again."

44

# 一本の　鉄路蟋蟀　なきわかる
## Ippon no　tetsuro kōrogi　naki wakaru

*Single row of tracks*
*separating the crickets*
*chirping on both sides.*

Composed 1940.
Gōra, in Hakone. Gōra is the terminal point of the mountain railway.
As I walked along the track, crickets were chirping on either side.
That single row of tracks divided the crickets on either side.

---

Season Word: *kōrogi*, "cricket." Autumn, animals.

*Vocabulary:*
- implied after *tetsuro* (lit. "iron road" → "train tracks") is something like *ni/ni yotte*, ("by/by means of").
- *naki* is from *naku* ("[an animal] cries/sings/calls," and *wakaru* means "be separated/divided/distinguished," so the two together mean something like "to be separated in [their]cries/crying."

蟋蟀が　深き地中を　覗き込む
Kōrogi ga　fukaki chichū o　nozokikomu

# A cricket peering
# intently into regions
# subterranean.

Composed 1940.
I was crouched on the ground where I could observe closely life on
the surface and came upon a cricket. That cricket was looking down a
hole deep into the earth. Even a cricket will do such a sad thing.

---

Season Word: *kōrogi*, "cricket." Autumn, animals.

*Vocabulary:*
- *fukaki* is the classical *-ki* form of the adjective *fukai* ("deep"), for directly modifying nouns.
- *chichū* is "earth/ground" plus "inside/interior," so *fukaki chichū* is literally "the deep earth interior" → "the depths of the earth."
- *nozoki* is from *nozoku* ("peep/peer into"), and the suffix *-komu* emphasizes that the action is directed "into" something.

# 機関車の　寒暮炎えつつ　湖わたる

*Kikansha no　　kanbo moe tsutsu　　umi wataru*

## *A winter evening —*
## *a flaming locomotive*
## *rides across the lake.*

Composed 1940.
Imagire, on Lake Hamana. A long iron bridge crosses the entrance of
the lake, and a locomotive went over it one winter evening. The
flames in the firebox shook. Roaring flames rode across the lake on a
winter evening.

---

Season Word: *kanbo*, "winter evening." Winter, season.

*Vocabulary:*
- *moe* is from *moeru* ("combust/burn"), and using the kanji 炎 (usually read *honoo*, the Japanese word for "flames") emphasizes the image of the flames rather than the simple fact that something is burning.
- *tsutsu* indicates that a second action is occurring "while/at the same time as" the first action takes place.
- the kanji 湖, whose standard reading is *mizuumi* ("lake"), makes it clear that *umi* here means "lake" rather than "sea/ocean."

活けし梅　　一枝強く　　壁に触る
*Ikeshi ume*　　*hitoeda tsuyoku*　　*kabe ni furu*

***Flowering plum branch
in an arrangement, poking
hard into a wall.***

Composed 1941.
Plum branches were arranged in a vase in the alcove. The branches
stuck out sharply, and one of them rubbed against the wall. To my
eyes that branch was poking hard into the wall.

---

Season Word: *ume*, "plum." Spring, plants.

*Vocabulary:*
- *ikeshi* is a classical equivalent of *iketa*, past form of *ikeru* ("arrange [flowers in a vase]").
- *furu* = modern *fureru* ("touch"), and *tsuyoku . . . furu* = "touch strongly" → "push/press/poke hard."

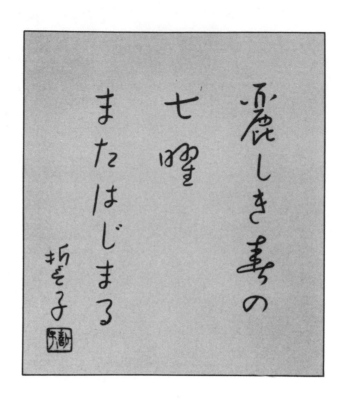

麗しき妻の
七瞳
またはじまる
哲之子

50

麗しき　春の七曜　またはじまる
*Uruwashiki　haru no shichiyō　mata hajimaru*

***Spring has come again,***
***with week after glorious week,***
***each of seven days.***

Composed 1941.
Spring brings us lovely days seven days a week. After seven glorious
spring days pass, the next seven days succeed. As long as spring
lasts, its lovely seven days come again and again.

---

◆　Season Word: *haru*, "spring." Spring, season.

*Vocabulary:*
- *uruwashiki* is the classical *-ki* form of *uruwashii* ("beautiful/lovely/glorious/ splendid").

ほふし蝉　こゑをさむるも　わが咫尺

*Hōshizemi*　　*koe osamuru mo*　　*waga shiseki*

# *A priest cicada*
# *comes to the end of his song*
# *right under my nose.*

Composed 1941.

A priest cicada began to sing in a tree very close by. When he had finished one phrase, he stopped singing. Still in that very near tree. I made a poem about the end of the song in order to recall the beginning.

---

Season Word: *hōshizemi*, "priest cicada." Autumn, animals.

*Vocabulary:*
- ほふし is the traditional spelling of *hōshi* ("monk/priest"), and をさむる is the traditional spelling/form of *osameru* ("finish/complete/put away").
- 咫尺 *shiseki* literally means "eight to ten inches" and implies "a very short distance/very close by."

*Other points of interest:*
- Japan is host to twenty to thirty species of cicada, which make summer a riot of sound. Their features are studied well by the people who dwell with them and know their songs.

52

驟雨来ぬ　　蝉は両眼　　濡らし啼く
*Shūu kinu*　　*semi wa ryōgan*　　*nurashi naku*

# *A sudden shower —*
# *cicadas go on singing,*
# *water in both eyes.*

Composed 1941.
Cicadas were singing in a tree. It suddenly started raining, but they
went on singing. They seemed to be singing with rain falling in their
eyes.

---

Season Word: *semi*, "cicada." Summer, animals.

*Vocabulary:*
- *shūu* = "sudden shower/cloudburst"
- *kinu* is a classical equivalent of *kita*, the past form of *kuru* ("comes").
- *nurashi* is essentially an abbreviated *-te* form of *nurasu* ("to wet/moisten"), and it functions like an adverb modifying *naku* ("[an animal] cries/sings/calls"): *ryōgan nurashi(te) naku* is literally "cry with both eyes wet."

碧揚羽　　通るを時の　　驕りとす
*Ao-ageha*　　*tōru o toki no*　　*ogori to su*

# *It made my hour*
# *elegant by passing by —*
# *a blue swallowtail.*

Composed 1941.
The blue swallowtail is a very beautiful shining blue against a black background. It is an exquisite butterfly. A blue swallowtail passed by and made my hour an exquisite hour.

---

Season Word: *ao-ageha*, "blue swallowtail." Spring, animals.

*Vocabulary:*
- *tōru* is a verb, "pass/go through," but marking it with *o*, for direct objects, effectively turns it into a noun ("a/the passing"), quite as if one of the usual nominalizers (*no*, *koto*) had been used.
- *ogori* is the noun form of *ogoru* ("do as one pleases/have one's way/be extravagant"), and *su* is the classical form of *suru* ("do/make"), so *(toki no) ogori to su* can be thought of literally as "make [the swallowtail's passing] my pleasure/extravagance (of the hour)" → "[the swallowtail's passing] made my (hour)."

つきぬけて　天上の紺　曼珠沙華
*Tsukinukete　tenjō no kon　manjushage*

# *Up into the sky*
## *a penetrating azure —*
### *red spider lily.*

Composed 1941.
It was a red spider lily. The sky was an autumnal blue — high into the sky, a penetrating blue. Under that blue sky stood that bright red flower.

---

Season Word: *manjushage*, "red spider lily" (*Lycoris radiata*). Autumn, plants.

*Vocabulary:*
- *tsukinukete* is from *tsukinukeru* ("penetrate/go all the way through").
- between *kon* ("deep blue") and *manjushage* ("red spider lily") is implied something like the particle *ni*, meaning "juxtaposed/set against."

雁のこゑ　すべて月下を　過ぎ終る

*Kari no koe*　　*subete gekka o*　　*sugiowaru*

### *Voices of wild geese —*
### *every one has now passed by,*
### *underneath the moon.*

Composed 1941.
The moon was shining in the sky. Birds were passing under it, calling to each other. It was a flock of wild geese. The voices of the wild geese all went by under the moon. One could tell by their voices when they had all passed by.

---

Season Word: *kari*, "wild geese." Autumn, animals.

*Vocabulary:*
- こゑ is the old spelling of こえ *koe* ("voice," or, with animals, "song/cry/call"). Like ゐ (see poem 26), ゑ belonged to the *wa* column of the kana chart and was originally pronounced *we*.
- *sugi* is from *sugiru* ("pass/go by"), and *owaru* ("end/finish") added to the stem of a verb means the action finishes/comes to an end, so *sugiowaru* = "finish passing."

雪敷きて　　海に近寄る　　こともなし
*Yuki shikite*　　*umi ni chikayoru*　　*koto mo nashi*


*A carpet of snow*
*keeping me from going close*
*to the ocean's edge.*


Composed 1941.
I lived in a house by the shore. Snow fell and accumulated between
my house and the ocean. I always went out to the ocean and watched
it, but the snow kept me away.

---

Season Word: *yuki*, "snow." Winter, celestial phenomena.

*Vocabulary:*
- *shikite* is the old *-te* form of *shiku* ("spread/lay out [like a carpet]").
- *umi ni chikayoru* is a complete thought/sentence ("[I] approach the sea") modify-
  ing *koto* ("thing/situation").
- *nashi* is the classical form of *nai* ("not exist"). The expression *koto ga aru/nai*
  means "[the described thing/situation] does/does not occur." Changing *ga* to *mo*
  adds emphasis: "doesn't even occur."

血潮濃き　水にしなほも　鰤洗ふ

*Chishio koki*　　*mizu ni shi nao mo*　　*buri arau*

# *Cleaning yellowtail*
# *in water turned vermilion*
# *by their flowing blood.*

Composed 1942.

In a fish store in a town by the sea, yellowtail were being cut up, producing bright red blood. The owner washed them in a tub of water. Though the water became blood red, the fish washed in it became clean. The blood was washed off with blood.

---

Season Word: *buri*, "yellowtail." Winter, animals.

*Vocabulary:*
- *koki* is the classical *-ki* form of the adjective *koi* ("be thick/dark/saturated with").
- *shi* is short for *shite*, the *-te* form of *suru*. The expression . . . *ni suru* could mean either "put/place into [the water]" or "make/turn into [blood-red water]," but the latter seems preferable here since the author's note implies that the water was clear at first.
- なほも is the old spelling of なおも *nao mo*, meaning "even still/and yet."
- 洗ふ is the old spelling of 洗う *arau* ("wash/rinse").

病快し　かげろふ砂を　手に握る

*Yamai yoshi*　　*kagerou suna o*　　*te ni nigiru*

## *Regaining my health,*
## *I seize upon a handful*
## *of shimmering sand.*

Composed 1942.
Spring had come, and my health showed signs of returning. I went
out on the beach, picked up sand that had been reflecting the sun, and
squeezed it, thus to receive the spirit of the sun in the sand.

---

Season Word: *kagerō*, "heat shimmer." Spring, celestial phenomena.

*Vocabulary:*
- 快し *yoshi* is more commonly read *kokoroyoshi*, equivalent to modern Japanese *kokoroyoi* ("pleasant/agreeable" or, in connection with illness, "is better/is getting better"). Reading it differently does not alter the meaning.
- かげろふ is the old spelling of かげろう *kagerou* ("to shimmer"), which refers to the effect seen in the air over sand/earth/asphalt on a hot day. The word occurs both as a noun and as a verb, but here it is a verb functioning as a modifier for *suna* ("sand"): "sand that shimmers/shimmering sand."

高きより　雪降り松に　沿ひ下る
*Takaki yori　yuki furi matsu ni　soi kudaru*

*From high in the sky,*
*the snow making its way down*
*following the pine.*

Composed 1942.
In the garden was a tall, erect pine. Snow began to descend parallel with the trunk of the tree. The snow fell like that because the trunk was so straight.

---

Season Word: *yuki*, "snow." Winter, celestial phenomena.

*Vocabulary:*
- *takaki* is the classical *-ki* form of the adjective *takai* ("high/tall"), which in this case makes the adjective function as a noun by implying something like *takaki tokoro*, "a high place."
- *yori* = "from"
- 沿ひ is the old spelling of 沿い *soi*, the stem form of *sou* ("be/go/run alongside of [something]"). The stem here is essentially an abbreviated *-te* form functioning as an adverb that modifies *kudaru* ("descends/drops/comes down").

紅くあかく　海のほとりに　梅を干す

*Akaku akaku*　　*umi no hotori ni*　　*ume o hosu*

## Crimson on crimson
### masses of plums spread to dry
### beside the ocean.

Composed 1942.
In houses by the sea, mats are spread on the shore to dry plums. I saw
the plums lying in masses of pure, pure crimson, and called them
"Crimson on crimson."

---

Season Word: *ume o hosu*, "to dry plums." Summer, life.

*Vocabulary:*
- *akaku* is the adverb form of *akai* ("red/crimson"), and *akaku akaku* implies something like *akaku akaku mieru*, "appears/can be seen red as red can be."

*Other points of interest:*
- the *umeboshi*, or dried/pickled plum, has long been a basic element in the Japanese diet. Its acid taste is said to give it many medicinal powers, including the fumigation of lunch boxes. A simple box lunch consisting of steamed white rice with a bright red *umeboshi* in the middle of it is known as a "rising sun lunch" because of its resemblance to the Japanese flag.

干梅の　　上来る酸の　　風絶えず
*Hoshi-ume no　　ue kuru san no　　kaze taezu*

### *An incessant wind*
### *blowing sour fragrances*
### *of plums spread to dry.*

Composed 1942.
Plums are drying on a mat. The wind blows over them in the direction of the house. It is a sour wind, passing incessantly over the drying plums.

---

Season Word: *hoshi-ume*, "drying plums." Summer, life.

*Vocabulary:*
- *umeboshi* is the name of the already dried/pickled plums, combining *ume* ("plum") and *hoshi* (the noun form of *hosu*, "dry"; *h* changes to *b* for euphony), but turning the combination around makes *hoshi-ume*, "plums that are drying" → "drying plums."
- the particle *o* has been omitted after *ue* ("above/over"); *hoshi-ume no ue (o) kuru* is a complete thought/sentence ("comes over the drying plums") modifying *san no kaze* ("acid/sour wind").
- *taezu* is a classical equivalent of *taenai*, the negative form of *taeru* ("cease/stop/break off"). The particle *ga* has been omitted after *kaze*.

蟋蟀の　　無明に海の　　いなびかり

*Kōrogi no*　　*mumyō ni umi no*　　*inabikari*

*A cricket crying*
*in darkness; on the ocean*
*lightning is flashing.*

Composed 1942.
Night has fallen. A blind cricket goes on chirping. In the offing,
lightning is flashing. The cricket cannot see it, but the lightning keeps
on flashing.

---

Season Word: *kōrogi*, "cricket." Autumn, animals.

*Vocabulary:*
- *ni* essentially means "and," in this case implying the two items are juxtaposed/set against each other in a kind of contrast.
- *mumyō* is literally "no light" → "darkness," so the poem simply says "The crickets' darkness and the ocean's lightning flashes." But since it is for their crying that crickets are known, the sound of their voices is implicit.

*Other points of interest:*
- there are 40 or so species of cricket in Japan. The Japanese like to keep insects in cages in their homes, where their voices add to the sense of bringing the garden indoors.

提げゆきし　百合の香ここに　とどまれる

*Sage yukishi*　　*yuri no ka koko ni*　　*todomareru*

## *The lily she held*
## *in her hand as she passed by*
## *left its fragrance here.*

Composed 1942.

When I was out in front of the house, someone went by holding a lily in her hand. The scent of the lily remained before me, filling the air. The scent of the lily remained here along the path she had taken.

---

Season Word: *yuri*, "lily." Summer, plants.

*Vocabulary:*
- *sage* is from *sageru*, which refers to holding/carrying something with one's hand dangling at one's side — such as a briefcase, a shopping bag with handles, or a small package.
- *yukishi* is equivalent to *itta*, the past form of *iku* ("go"), so *sage yukishi* means "go/pass [by] while holding" → "carry past."
- *todomareru* is a classical equivalent of *todomatte-iru* ("remains in place/behind") from *todomaru* ("halt/remain behind").

春水と　行くを止むれば　流れ去る
Shunsui to　　yuku o yamureba　　nagare saru

# When I stopped walking
## along with the spring freshet,
### it kept flowing on.

Composed 1943.
I walked beside a stream of spring runoff, but stopped walking along the way. The stream had lost its fellow traveller, meaning me, but kept flowing on alone. Fate had made me and the spring freshet fellow travelers.

---

Season Word: *shunsui*, "spring freshet." Spring, topography.

*Vocabulary:*
- *yuku* (= *iku*, "go") is a verb, but *o* effectively turns it into a noun ("going/the act of going" → "walking"). See page 54.
- *yamureba* is the classical *-ba* form, meaning "when –," of *yameru* ("stop/cease/quit [something]").
- *nagare*, from *nagareru* ("flow") combines with *saru* ("go away/depart") to mean "wash/flow away" → "flow on."

鷹の羽を　拾ひて持てば　風集ふ
*Taka no ha o*　　*hiroite moteba*　　*kaze tsudou*

## *Holding in my hand*
## *a hawk's feather, as the winds*
## *gather around it.*

Composed 1943.

I picked up a falcon's feather on the beach. It was a beautiful feather with white spots. When I held it up, the winds noticed and assembled around it. The feather was beautiful even to the winds.

---

✦　Season Word: *taka*, "hawk." Winter, animals.

*Vocabulary:*
- 拾ひて is the classical *-te* form of *hirou* ("pick up"), and *moteba* is from *motsu* ("hold"), so *hiroite moteba* means "when I picked [something] up and held it."
- 集ふ is the traditional spelling of 集う *tsudou*, a word that has now been largely supplanted in common usage by 集まる *atsumaru* ("[something] gathers/clusters/flocks together").

伊吹嶽　　殘雪天に　　離れ去る
*Ibukidake*　　*zansetsu ten ni*　　*hanare saru*

***Ibukidake —***

***the last snow has departed***

***off into heaven.***

Composed 1943.

From Ise, I could see Mount Ibuki off to the north. Snow covered the mountain in the winter, but began to melt away from the foot of the mountain in spring. The snow on the summit lingered to the last. Then that snow disappeared. The last snow rose into heaven.

---

Season Word: *zansetsu*, "remaining snow." Spring, topography.

*Vocabulary:*
- 嶽, *-dake* or *-take*, meaning "peak/mountain," is the last element in the names of many Japanese mountains.
- *zansetsu* is written with kanji meaning "left over/remaining" and "snow" → "last snow."
- *hanare saru* is literally "separates and goes away" → "departs."

城を出し　落花一片　いまもとぶ

*Shiro o deshi*　　*rakka ippen*　　*ima mo tobu*

# *It is flying still —*
# *the cherry petal I saw*
# *depart the castle.*

Composed 1944.
Cherry trees were blooming above Matsuzaka Castle. As I came out,
I looked up at the sky and saw a cherry petal flying out of the castle.
After walking a little, I looked up again and saw the same cherry
petal, still flying.

---

✦　Season Word: *rakka*, "fallen petal." Spring, plants.

*Vocabulary:*
- *deshi* is a classical Japanese equivalent of *deta*, the past form of *deru* ("exit/go out/come out"). *Shiro o deshi* is a complete thought/sentence ("came out of the castle") modifying *rakka ippen* ("fallen flower's single petal").
- *ima* = "now" and *ima mo* = "even now."

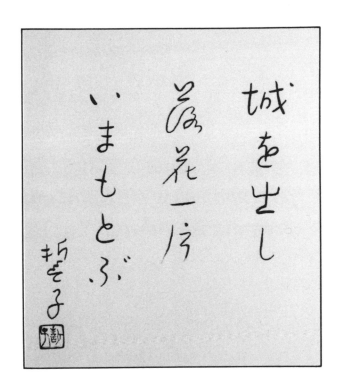

城を出し
藤花一房
いまもとぶ

哲子

この崖に　わがイつかぎり　蟹ひそむ
*Kono gake ni　waga tatsu kagiri　kani hisomu*

## *As long as I stand here upon this cliff, the crabs remain in hiding.*

Composed 1944.

I was standing on a cliff. There were crab holes in the cliff below me, which the crabs normally went in and out of. Because I was standing there, they remained in hiding, waiting for me to depart.

---

Season Word: *kani*, "crab." Summer, animals.

*Vocabulary:*
- *waga* = "I/me."
- *kagiri* after a verb implies "so long as [the action continues]."
- *hisomu* = "be in hiding/conceal oneself/lie low."

みめよくて　田植の笠に　指を添ふ

*Mime yokute*　　*taue no kasa ni*　　*yubi o sou*

# A beautiful girl
## in a rice-planting bonnet,
## fingering the brim.

Composed 1944.
She was a rice-planting girl. She was beautiful, with a straw rice-planting hat on her head. When she met me on the road, she touched her fingers to the brim of her bonnet. It was a gesture that showed her awareness of her own beauty.

---

Season Word: *taue*, "rice-planting." Summer, life.

*Vocabulary:*
- *mimeyokute* is from *mimeyoi* ("comely/beautiful/fair [maiden]"). The *-te* form implies a cause-effect relationship between this and *yubi o sou* ("touches [her] fingers [to]"): she touches the brim of her hat *because* she knows/is self-conscious of her beauty.
- 添ふ *sou* here is equivalent to modern *soeru* ("add/attach/affix to") → "touch."

*Other points of interest:*
- rice-planting festivals are held throughout Japan in June. The farmers dress in colorful garments, including broad-brimmed hats, and sing songs to drum accompaniment as they stand in flooded fields and press young plants into the soft earth.

71

崖攀づる　蟹や吾より　高くなり

*Gake yozuru*　　*kani ya ware yori*　　*takaku nari*

***A crab on a cliff***
***continuing its scramble***
***higher up than I.***

Composed 1944.
It was a crab hill. One of the crabs began to climb from the bottom.
He climbed to the height of my eyes, and then continued scrambling
even higher. I kept watching that crab surpassing me in height.

Season Word: *kani*, "crab." Summer, animals.

*Vocabulary:*
- *yozuru* is a classical Japanese equivalent of *yojiru* or *yojinoboru* ("clamber/
  scramble up").
- *ya* in haiku is a *kireji*, or "cutting word," which generally has the effect of divid-
  ing the poem into two parts, as with a long dash or colon; in many cases it also
  gives the feeling of an exclamation.
- *nari* is a form of *naru* ("become"), so *takaku nari* means "becomes/became
  higher."

水甕に　　浮べる蟻の　　影はなく
*Mizugame ni*　　*ukaberu ari no*　　*kage wa naku*

**A jar of water**
**with an ant floating in it,**
**casting no shadow.**

Composed 1944.

An ant has fallen into a jar of water and floats on the surface. An ant is a small living thing, but it should cast a shadow. The water is very deep, and I cannot see his shadow. I cannot see the shadow that should be there.

---

Season Word: *ari*, "ant." Summer, animals.

*Vocabulary:*
- *ukaberu* is equivalent to modern *ukanda*, the past form of *ukabu* ("float"). *mizugame ni ukaberu* is a complete thought/sentence ("floats in the water jar") modifying *ari* ("ant"), and that entire phrase in turn modifies *kage* ("shadow"): "the shadow of the ant floating in the water jar."
- *naku* is a form of *nai* ("not exist").

やはらかき　稚子の昼寝の　つづきけり

*Yawarakaki* 　　*chigo no hirune no* 　　*tsuzukikeri*

# A soft little mass
# of infant taking a nap,
# snoozing on and on.

Composed 1944.
A very young child who came to play at my house is taking a nap. A soft little lump of flesh is taking a nap, from which he is not easily awakened. A soft nap!

Season Word: *hirune*, "nap." Summer, life.

*Vocabulary:*
- *yawarakaki* is the classical *-ki* form of the adjective *yawarakai* ("soft").
- *chigo* = "infant/baby."
- *tsuzukikeri* is a classical exclamatory form of *tsuzuku* ("continue").

たらたらと　　縁に滴る　　いなびかり
*Taratara-to*　　*en ni shitataru*　　*inabikari*


***Falling drop by drop,***
***speckling the veranda —***
***flashes of lightning.***


Composed 1944.
When I was on the veranda, lightning flashed and illuminated the
veranda. It seemed to me that the lightning was falling like water and
wetting the floor. I thought the lightning was drops of water.

Season Word: *inabikari*, "lightning." Summer, celestial phenomena.

*Vocabulary:*
- *taratara* is a mimetic word representing the effect of liquid dripping/trickling
  continuously, and *taratara-to* is its adverb form.
- *shitataru* is a verb meaning "to drip," so *taratara-to shitataru* = "drip in a *tara-
  tara* manner."
- since *shitataru* normally is used of liquids, it can imply *ame* ("rain"), but Seishi
  makes clear in his note that he intends a more figurative meaning, with *taratara-
  to en ni shitataru* ("dripping *taratara* on the veranda") directly modifying *ina-
  bikari* ("lightning flashes").

あはれ蟻　　家の柱を　　高あがる
*Aware ari*　　*ie no hashira o*　　*takaagaru*

***Miserable ant***
***climbing up a house pillar***
***higher and higher.***

Composed 1944.
Ants like to climb to high places. One came off the ground outside
and into my house, and, finding a pillar in the way, began to climb it.
I watched the ant climbing higher and higher.

Season Word: *ari*, "ant." Summer, animals.

*Vocabulary:*
- *aware* is essentially an expression of one's deep feelings for something, often implying pity (see poem 21). Here the word does not modify *ari*, but instead functions as an opening exclamation, "Oh, how miserable it is!" The poem then goes on to describe what brought on this exclamation.
- *taka* here implies *takaku*, the adverb form of *takai* ("high"), and *agaru* means "rise/climb," so *takaagaru* = "climb high/higher."

月光に　障子をかたく　さしあはす

*Gekkō ni　　shōji o kataku　　sashiawasu*

# Screening the moonlight,
## sliding doors brought together
### firmly into place.

Composed 1944.

It was a bright, moonlit night. The paper doors, tightly drawn, were pure white. It was as if the doors had been brought together to keep out the moonlight.

Season Word: *gekkō*, "moonlight." Autumn, celestial phenomena.

*Vocabulary:*
- *kataku* is the adverb form of *katai* ("hard/firm") → "firmly/tightly."
- *sashi* is from *sasu*, used to refer to the closing of doors/windows/etc., and *awasu* is a classical equivalent of *awaseru* ("put/set together"), so *sashiawasu* means "draw [sliding doors] together."

仲秋や　　漁火は月より　　遠くして
*Chūshū ya*　　*gyoka wa tsuki yori*　　*tōku shite*

# *Mid-autumn season —*
# *fishing lights in the distance,*
# *farther than the moon.*

Composed 1944.

The mid-autumn moon rides in the sky. Fishing lights shine dimly in the distance. The dim fishing lights seem to be further away than the moon — poetic reality.

---

Season Word: *chūshū*, "mid-autumn." Autumn, season.

*Vocabulary:*
- under the old lunar calendar, autumn was the seventh, eighth, and ninth months, and *chūshū*, literally "middle autumn" referred to the eighth month, or, more specifically, to the full moon in the middle of the eighth month.
- *ya* in haiku is a *kireji*, or "cutting word," which generally has the effect of dividing the poem into two parts, as with a long dash or colon; in many cases it also gives the feeling of an exclamation.
- *tōku shite* here is essentially equivalent to the *-te* form of *tōi* ("far/distant"), and it has the effect of an exclamation.

78

俯向きて　　鳴く蟋蟀の　　こと思ふ
*Utsumukite*　　*naku kōrogi no*　　*koto omou*

## *Thinking about him:*
## *a cricket, chirping away,*
## *looking at the ground.*

Composed 1944.
I can hear a cricket chirping. As I listen to him, I imagine his posture.
Of course he is looking down as he sings.

Season Word: *kōrogi*, "cricket." Autumn, animals.

*Vocabulary:*
- *utsumukite* is the classical *-te* form of *utsumuku* ("lie/be face down"). The *-te* form here allows the word to modify *naku* ("cry/sing/chirp"). *Utsumukite naku* is a complete thought/sentence ("sing face down") modifying *kōrogi* ("cricket").
- . . . *no koto (o) omou* is an expression meaning "[I] think about . . ." 思ふ is the old spelling for 思う *omou*.

海に出て　　木枯帰る　　ところなし
*Umi ni dete　　kogarashi kaeru　　tokoro nashi*

*Once over the sea,*
*winter winds can no longer*
*return home again.*

Composed 1944.
The winter winds come down off the mountains, cross the plain, and, once out to sea, they are gone. They do not return to Japan. The winter winds of Japan lose their nationality.

---

◆　Season Word: *kogarashi*, "winter wind." Winter, celestial phenomena.

*Vocabulary:*
* *kogarashi* literally means "tree witherer" and implies "the wind that leaves the trees bare" → "winter wind." Placing *kogarashi* after *umi ni dete* ("goes out to sea") is inverted syntax. Normal order would be *kogarashi wa umi ni dete . . .* ("the winter wind goes out to sea and . . .").

*Other points of interest:*
* in addition to its surface meaning, this poem refers to the World War II tactic — which Americans associate with the word *kamikaze* — of sending bombing planes out over the Pacific with only enough fuel to reach their targets. Elsewhere Seishi has described the poem as written "also to mourn the victims of a tragic wartime practice."

80

# せりせりと　薄氷杖の　なすままに

*Seriseri-to*　　　*usurai tsue no*　　*nasu mama ni*

***With a crackling sound,***
***the thin ice allows my cane***
***to have its own way.***

Composed 1945.

A thin sheet of ice had formed. I stuck my cane in it and drew a circle. The ice crackled as it broke. It was the sound of the ice allowing the cane to do whatever it wished.

---

Season Word: *usurai*, "thin ice." Spring, topography.

*Vocabulary:*
- *seriseri* usually represents an effect of "busy-ness/unsettledness/restlessness," and in this case is intended as an onomatopoeia for the sound of the cane breaking up the thin ice. Adding *-to* makes it an adverb.
- *usurai*, usually written 薄ら氷, means "thin ice."
- *nasu* = "do."
- *mama* = "as is" and *ni* makes it an adverb, "in an as-is manner" — i.e., allowing whatever happens to happen, without resisting/attempting to prevent it → *(tsue no) nasu mama ni* = "allowing (the cane) to do whatever it pleases."

土堤を外れ　枯野の犬と　なりゆけり

*Dote o sore*　　*kareno no inu to*　　*nari yukeri*

# *A riverbank dog*
## *moves off the bank and becomes*
### *a withered-field dog.*

Composed 1945.
A dog running on a riverbank descends and runs along a path through a withered field. Thus, by a change in terrain, the "riverbank dog" becomes a "withered-field dog."

---

Season Word: *kareno*, "field of withered grass." Winter, topography.

*Vocabulary:*
- *sore* is from *soreru* ("swerve/veer off").
- *nari yukeri* is equivalent to modern *natte itta*, the *-te* form of *naru* ("become") and past form of *iku* ("go"). *Natte itta* often implies a progressive change ("became more and more . . ."), and here it gives the feeling that the change took several moments rather than being instantaneous.

# 天よりも　かがやくものは　蝶の翅

*Ten yori mo　　kagayaku mono wa　　chō no hane*

## *The butterfly's wings*
## *have a sheen even brighter*
## *than the sky above.*

Composed 1945.

A white butterfly flies in the spring sky. The sky is shining, and the butterfly shines too. Reflecting the spring sun on its white wings, the butterfly shines even brighter than the sky.

---

◆ Season Word: *chō*, "butterfly." Spring, animals.

*Vocabulary:*
- *ten* = "the heavens/the sky."
- *yori mo* = "even more than."
- *ten yori mo kagayaku* is a complete thought/sentence ("shines brighter than the sky") modifying *mono* ("thing").

開け置きし　玻璃戸直ちに　蝶を見る
*Ake okishi*　*harido tadachi ni*　*chō o miru*

## *An open window*
## *through which I look directly*
## *at a butterfly.*

Composed 1945.
A window stood open, and a butterfly passed by outside. I could look directly at it, without the mediation of the glass. The butterfly and I, directly linked.

---

◆　Season Word: *chō*, "butterfly." Spring, animals.

*Vocabulary:*
- *ake okishi* is equivalent to modern *akete oita*, the *-te* form of *akeru* ("open [something]") followed by the past form of *oku* ("set down/leave"). A *-te* form plus *oku* makes an expression meaning "do (the action) and leave things that way."
- *hari*, originally referring to "crystal," is an elegant/poetic (and now rather archaic sounding) word for "glass." *Do* (or *to* — in combinations, *t* changes to *d* for euphony) basically means "opening/gate," so it can be either a window or a door; but *garasudo* (or in this case *harido*) most often refers to "windows," and here the context suggests "window" as well.

84

少年の　　ごとし梅の実を　　食めば酸し
*Shōnen no*　　*gotoshi ume no mi o*　　*hameba sushi*

## *Chewing on a plum:*
## *sour taste making me feel*
## *like a boy again.*

Composed 1945.

I bit into a plum, and it tasted sour. The sour taste was the same as
that I knew when I was a boy. Carried back by the sour taste of the
plum, I became a boy again.

---

Season Word: *ume no mi*, "plum." Summer, plants.

*Vocabulary:*
- *gotoshi* is a classical word meaning "is/are like," so *shōnen no gotoshi* means "[I]
  am like a boy."
- *hameba* ("when I eat/chew") is from *hamu* ("eat/feed on").
- *sushi* is a classical adjective equivalent to modern *suppai* ("sour").

*Other points of interest:*
- the pickled plum, or *umeboshi*, has a special place among Japanese tastes. See
  page 61.

紫蘇壷を　　深淵覗く　ごとくする
*Shisotsubo o　　shin'en nozoku　　gotoku suru*

# *Taking a quick look*
# *into a pickling jar,*
# *into an abyss.*

Composed 1945.
I looked into a jar of pickling plums. The jar was filled with the dark red juice made by the leaves of beefsteak plants. The color reminded me of a deep chasm. Looking into the pickle jar was like looking into an abyss.

---

Season Word: *shiso*, "pickling herb." Summer, plants.

*Vocabulary:*
- *shiso* is known in English as "beefsteak plant," so *shisotsubo* is literally "beefsteak plant jar" → "pickling jar." *O* in this case means "[do] to/with [the jar]."
- *nozoku* = "peep/peer into," and *shin'en nozoku* = "peer into a deep abyss."
- *gotoku* is the adverb form of the classical *gotoshi* ("is like"), so *gotoku suru* is "do like/as if [peering into an abyss]."

*Other points of interest:*
- the red *shiso* leaf is used as a pickling herb both for its flavor and its color. It is also used as a garnish and a seasoning for cooked dishes. Western diners have mentioned tasting it in their pesto.

# 冷水を　　湛ふ水甕の　　底にまで

*Reisui o*　　*tatau mizugame no*　　*soko ni made*

## *A water vessel*
## *brimming full of cool water*
## *down to the bottom.*

Composed 1945.

A water vessel is filled to the surface with cool water. As I see it, the vessel is filled to the surface of the water, but the water goes all the way to the bottom. A stack of cool water.

---

Season Word: *reisui*, "cool water." Summer, topography.

*Vocabulary:*
- 湛ふ is the old form of 湛える *tataeru* ("contain/be filled to the brim with [a liquid]"). In this case the form creates a full stop; it does not modify *mizugame* ("water jar/vessel").
- *soko* = "the bottom/the depths"
- *ni* = "to" and *made* = "until"; the two particles together give the feeling of "even all the way down to."

87

炎天の　遠き帆やわが　こころの帆

Enten no　　tōki ho ya wa ga　　kokoro no ho

***Sails in scorching heat***
***in the offing are the sails***
***within my spirit.***

Composed 1945.
I can see sails in the offing under a blazing sun. Living near the
shore, I often see white sails in the offing and carry them in my
heart. The white sails in the offing under a blazing sun are real,
while the white sails within my heart are not — the consonance of
the real and the unreal.

---

✦　Season Word: *enten*, "scorching heat." Summer, celestial phenomena.

*Vocabulary:*
- *tōki* is the classical *-ki* form of the adjective *tōi* ("far/distant").
- *ya* in haiku is a *kireji*, or "cutting word," which generally has the effect of divid-
  ing the poem into two parts, as with a long dash or colon; in many cases it also
  gives the feeling of an exclamation.
- *waga* is equivalent to *watashi no* ("my/mine").

颱風の　　あとや日光　正しくて
*Taifū no*　　*ato ya nikkō*　　*tadashikute*

# *After the typhoon,*
## *the beaming of the sun's rays,*
## *undeviating.*

Composed 1945.
The heavens were thrown into confusion by a typhoon. After the
typhoon, the heavens returned to normal. The sun's rays beat
directly down. Unimpeded by the typhoon, the sun's rays are direct
once more.

---

Season Word: *taifū*, "typhoon." Autumn, celestial phenomena.

*Vocabulary:*
- *ya* is a *kireji* ("cutting word") dividing the poem into two parts, and giving the feeling of an exclamation.
- *tadashikute* is the *-te* form of *tadashii* ("be correct/right/proper"). Using the *-te* form implies "(the sunshine) is correct/normal (again), and . . ." The poet leaves the rest unsaid, but the exclamatory particle *ya* provides a fairly clear indication of how the poet feels.

なきやみて　　なほ天を占む　　法師蝉
*Nakiyamite*　　*nao ten o shimu*　　*hōshizemi*

## *The priest cicada*
## *stops singing; his voice goes on*
## *filling the heavens.*

Composed 1945.
While the priest cicada was in song, his voice filled the heavens.
When he stopped singing, his voice was gone, but I could still hear
it, pervading the sky. Not the real voice, but the unreal voice!

---

Season Word: *hōshizemi*, "priest cicada." Autumn, animals.

*Vocabulary:*
- *naki* is from *naku* ("cry/sing/call") and *yamite* is the classical *-te* form of *yamu* ("end/cease/stop"); *nakiyamu* = "stops crying."
- なほ is the traditional spelling of なお *nao* ("and even so/even still").
- 占む is the classical form of 占める *shimeru* ("occupy/hold/fill"). Since it is the sentence-final form, it can be thought of as functioning like a colon here.

鶫死して　　翅拡ぐるに　　任せたり
*Tsugumi shishite*　　*hane hiroguru ni*　　*makasetari*

## *The thrush is dead now,*
## *leaving wings for anyone*
## *to spread at his will.*

Composed 1945.
A friend gave me a thrush he had shot, and I tried to open its wings.
I was able to spread them just as I wished. Though he was dead, he
gave himself up to me, to do with as I pleased.

---

Season Word: *tsugumi*, "thrush." Autumn, animals.

*Vocabulary:*
- *shishite* is the *-te* form of *shisuru*, which may be described as a literary equivalent of *shinu* ("die").
- *hiroguru* is a classical form of *hirogeru* ("spread/unfold").
- *makasetari* is a classical equivalent of *makasete-iru*, the progressive ("is –ing") form of *makaseru* ("leave to/entrust/give charge of").

# 寒き夜の　オリオンに杖　挿し入れむ

*Samuki yo no　　Orion ni tsue　　sashi-iremu*

## *It is a cold night;*
## *I wish to extend my cane*
## *into Orion.*

Composed 1946.

One cold night, I got my cane and went for a walk. Orion was shining in the sky, like a basin full of water. I wanted to thrust my cane into it.

---

Season Word: *samuki yo*, "cold night." Winter, season.

*Vocabulary:*
- *samuki* is the classical *-ki* form of the adjective *samui* ("cold").
- *sashi* is from *sasu* ("pierce/stab") and *iremu* (the final *u* is silent) is a classical equivalent of *iretai*, the volitional ("want to") form of *ireru* ("put in/insert"): *(tsue) sashi-iremu* = "want to thrust (my cane) into."

虹のぼり　ゆき中天を　くだりゆき
*Niji nobori*　　*yuki chūten o*　　　*kudari yuki*

## *The rainbow curves up*
## *to the middle of the sky,*
## *then curves down again.*

Composed 1945.
A rainbow hung low in the sky. I followed its arch with my eyes. It curved gently up, reached a low apogee, and curved gently down again. I had followed a rainbow from beginning to end.

---

◆　Season Word: *niji,* "rainbow." Summer, celestial phenomena.

*Vocabulary:*
- *nobori yuki* is from *noboru* ("rise/climb") and *iku/yuku* ("go"), so it is like saying "– go/goes climbing." *Kudari* means "fall/descend," so *kudari yuki* is like "– go/ goes down."
- *chūten* suggests both "middle of the sky" and "in/through the sky."

93

夕焼けて　西の十万　億土透く

*Yūyakete*　　*nishi no jūman*　　*-okudo suku*

# *In the afterglow,*
## *ten trillion miles of heaven*
### *penetrating through.*

Composed 1946.
The western sky was crimson in the afterglow. The sky was transparent; one could see forever, even the ten trillion miles west to the Pure Land. A sky serene in the afterglow.

---

✦ Season Word: *yūyake*, "afterglow." Summer, celestial phenomena.

*Vocabulary:*
- *yūyake* ("sunset/afterglow") is a combination of *yū* ("evening") and the noun form of *yakeru* ("burn"), and the word usually occurs as a noun. But using the *-te* form of *yakeru* makes this instance a verb, meaning literally "the evening has burned, and . . ." → "the evening sky glows with the sunset, and . . ."
- *jūman-okudo* (literally, "land that is ten trillion miles away") is another name for the "Pure Land/Paradise" of Amida Buddhism, traditionally said to be in the West. Though it does not disrupt the syllable count, this word forces the last two lines to be run together.
- *suku* = "be transparent."

われありと　　思ふ鵙啼き　　過ぐるたび
*Ware ari to*　　*omou mozu naki*　　*suguru tabi*

# *In the moments when*
# *a shrike flies past me singing,*
# *I know that I am.*

Composed 1946.

A shrike flew past me, singing in piercing tones. I wasn't thinking of anything, but when I heard the sharp voice of the shrike, I suddenly became aware of my own existence, as I do now whenever a shrike passes me in voice.

---

Season Word: *mozu*, "shrike." Autumn, animals.

*Vocabulary:*
- *ware* = "I/me" and *ari* is the classical verb of existence, "am/is/are/exists," so *ware ari* means "I am/I exist."
- *naki* (from *naku*, "cry/sing/call") plus *suguru* (= modern *suguru*, "pass/go by") modifies *tabi* ("time/occasion") → "each time [it] goes by singing/in voice."
- normal syntax would be *Mozu naki suguru tabi (ni) ware ari to omou.*

*Other points of interest:*
- the shrike, or butcher bird, is known everywhere for his predatory habits and his method of storing his kills on thorns and branches and even barbed wire. The bird has a distinguished place in the haiku literature and is said to herald autumn with his first impaling.

極く近く　海を湛へて　薄氷
*Goku chikaku　umi o tataete　usugōri*

# A thin sheet of ice
# and, not very far away,
# the spreading ocean.

Composed 1947.
I was living near the ocean. A thin layer of ice had formed on a pool quite close to the shore. The icy area was small and tranquil. The ocean was vast and moving. That contrast.

---

Season Word: *usugōri*, "thin ice." Spring, topography.

*Vocabulary:*
- *goku* = "very/extremely" and *chikaku* is the adverb form of *chikai* ("close/near"), modifying *tataete*.
- 湛へて is the traditional spelling of *tataete*, the *-te* form of both classical *tatau* and modern *tataeru*, meaning "contain/brim with [a liquid]." *Chikaku umi o tataete* is literally like "with the ocean brimming nearby."
- 薄氷 has the same meaning whether read *usugōri*, *usurai*, or *usurahi* (see page 81).

氷結の　　上上雪の　　降り積る

*Hyōketsu no*　　*ue ue yuki no*　　*furi tsumoru*

# *On congealing ice,*
## *snow is falling, piling up*
## *higher and higher.*

Composed 1947.

The water has frozen into a sheet of ice. Snow is piling up on top of it. The snow is piling up on the sheet of ice. The snow keeps falling and piling higher and higher.

Season Word: *yuki*, "snow." Winter, celestial phenomena.

*Vocabulary:*
- *hyōketsu* can refer either to the process of ice forming, or to the ice that has formed.
- *– no ue* means "on top of." Doubling *ue* is quite unconventional, a little like saying "on top of the on top of" → "[piles] higher and higher."
- *no* after *yuki* ("snow") is like *ga*, marking the subject.

鷺とんで　直ぐ雪嶺の　上に出づ

*Sagi tonde*　　*sugu setsurei no*　　*ue ni izu*

### *Heron taking off,*
### *in a moment hovering*
### *over snowy peak.*

Composed 1947.
A heron took off from the base of a snowy mountain. It climbed to the top of the mountain and into the sky above. The speed of that climb.

---

◆　Season Word: *setsurei*, "snowy peak." Winter, topography.

*Vocabulary:*
- *tonde* is the *-te* form of *tobu* ("fly").
- *sugu* = "immediately/right away."
- *izu* is the classical word for *deru* ("come out/go out/exit"). *Ue ni izu* is like saying "came/went out over the top of."

波にのり　波にのり鵜の　さびしさは

*Nami ni nori　nami ni nori u no　sabishisa wa*

**Riding on the waves,**
**riding on the waves —**
**the cormorant's loneliness.**

Composed 1947.
A cormorant was floating on Ise Bay. A wave would come, and he
would be lifted by it; then the next wave would come, and he would
be lifted by it. That solitary cormorant seemed so lonely.

---

Season Word: *u*, "cormorant." Summer, animals.

*Vocabulary:*
- *nori* is the stem form of *noru* ("ride on"). Using the stem form here implies something more will follow: "rides on the waves, and . . ." Repeating the phrase, still in the stem form, gives the feeling of "rides and rides and . . ." — as if it goes on endlessly.
- *sabishisa* is the noun form of *sabishii* ("lonely"). *Wa* marks this as the topic, as if something more will be said about it, but in this case the topic itself says all that needs to be said.

行く雁の　啼くとき宙の　感ぜられ

*Yuku kari no　　naku toki chū no　　kanzerare*

## *The call of wild geese returning: the impression of the sense of space.*

Composed 1947.
A flock of geese was returning north, their voices audible as they passed over. As I heard their voices, that flock of geese became part of my consciousness. At the same time, I became conscious of the space through which they were passing.

---

Season Word: *kari*, "wild geese." Autumn, animals.

*Vocabulary:*
- *no*, in each case, marks a subject: *yuku kari* (lit., "the going geese" → "the returning geese") is the subject of *naku* ("cry/sing/call"), and *yuku kari no naku* is a complete thought/sentence ("the returning geese call") modifying *toki* ("time"): "the time when the returning geese call" → "when the returning geese call."
- *kanzerare* is from *kanzu*, the classical equivalent of *kanjiru* ("to feel/sense/be aware of"). It is a passive form of the verb ("[sense of space] is felt [by me]"), and also implies that the feeling arose spontaneously/naturally, of its own accord, when the speaker neither intended nor expected it.

螢獲て　　少年の指　　みどりなり
*Hotaru ete*　　*shōnen no yubi*　　*midori nari*

# *Pinching the firefly*
# *he has caught, the boy's fingers*
# *go green at the tips.*

Composed 1947.
I was invited to a firefly hunt. A boy in the party caught a firefly and
held it between his thumb and index finger in order to put it in the
cage. The green glow of the firefly turned the boy's thumb and
fingertip to green.

---

✦ Season Word: *hotaru*, "firefly." Summer, animals.

*Vocabulary:*
- *ete* is the *-te* form of *eru*, generally meaning "obtain/acquire." The kanji 獲 im-
  plies more specifically, "capture/take in a hunt."
- *no* here is possessive.
- *nari* is a classical equivalent of *da/desu* ("is/are"), so *midori nari* means "is/are
  green."

悲しさの　　極みに誰か　枯木折る

*Kanashisa no*　　*kiwami ni tare ka*　　*kareki oru*

## *At the deepest point*
## *of grief, somebody nearby*
## *breaks a withered branch.*

Composed 1947.
I had suffered a terrible loss and was at the deepest point of grief.
When I felt I could bear it no longer, someone outside the house
snapped a dead, withered branch. That sad sound made my grief —
already at its deepest — somehow even deeper.

---

Season Word: *kareki*, "withered tree." Winter, plants.

*Vocabulary:*
- *kanashisa* is a noun form of *kanashii* ("sad/sorrowful").
- *kiwami* is a noun meaning "the most extreme point," so *kanashisa no kiwami n*
  is "at the extremity/deepest point of sadness/grief."
- *tare ka* is the classical form of *dareka* ("someone/anyone").
- the particle *o* is understood after *kareki* ("withered tree/branch"), which is the
  object of the verb *oru* ("break/snap in two").

102

秋の暮
み中もまた
暗くなる

　　　哲を子

秋の暮　水中もまた　暗くなる

*Aki no kure    suichū mo mata    kuraku naru*

## An autumn twilight —
## the depths of the water, too,
## darkening with it.

Composed 1947.
I was taking a walk by the water in the autumn twilight. The twilight darkened the air around me and even the depths of the water. After making the air dark, the shades of twilight entered the water, darkening it as well — or so it seemed to me.

---

Season Word: *aki*, "autumn." Autumn, season.

*Vocabulary:*
- *kure* = "dusk/nightfall," and *aki no kure* = "an autumn twilight."
- *suichū* combines "water" and "within/inside" to make a word that can mean either "in/within the water" or "underwater," depending on the context.
- *mo* and *mata* both mean "too/also/as well," and using them together emphasizes the inclusiveness, something like, "and also even within the water, too . . . "
- *kuraku naru* = "becomes dark."

除夜零時　過ぎてこころの　華やぐも

*Joya reiji*　　*sugite kokoro no*　　*hanayagu mo*

# *How the heart exults*
# *on the eve of the new year,*
# *as midnight passes.*

Composed 1948.

The boundary between the outgoing year and the new year is 24:00 on the last day of the year. When the old year passes that boundary, the year changes into the new year. My heart, too, suddenly feels the splendor.

---

Season Word: *joya*, "New Year's eve." Winter, season.

*Vocabulary:*

- *joya* refers specifically to the night of New Year's Eve. *Reiji* is literally "zero hour" → "midnight."
- *sugite* is the *-te* form of *sugiru* ("pass/passes").
- *no* is like *ga*, marking *kokoro* ("heart") as the subject of *hanayagu*.
- *hanayagu* means "become(s) gay/bright/splendid," from *hanayaka(-na)*, "gay/bright/splendid." Here it suggests the splendor that comes from newness, and from the feeling of renewal.

106

水枕　　中を寒柝　うち通る
Mizumakura　　naka o kantaku　　uchitōru

*Frigid night warning*
*from the watchman clatters through*
*my water pillow.*

Composed 1948.
I had a high fever and lay with my head on a water pillow. The sound
of wooden clappers entered and came through the pillow. The
clappers warned people to be careful of fires on this cold night.

---

Season Word: *kantaku*, "the sound of the watchman's warning clappers." Winter, life.

*Vocabulary:*
- with the particle *no* omitted, it is as if *mizumakura* ("water pillow") has been set off with a colon, but the meaning is essentially the same: *mizumakura no naka* = "inside the water pillow," and *mizumakura (no) naka o . . . tōru* = "pass/go through the water pillow."
- *kantaku* refers to the sound of the wooden clappers used by watchmen on winter nights to remind residents to check their stoves and charcoal braziers before going to bed.
- *uchi-* is a verb prefix with little if any meaning. Sometimes it can be considered mildly emphatic, but often its purpose is purely rhythmical.

かの雪嶺　信濃の国の　遠さ以て

*Kano yukine　Shinano no kuni no　tōsa mote*

## *That snowy mountain*
## *has in it all the distance*
## *off to Shinano.*

Composed 1948.

I can see a snowy mountain a long way from my house. I have been told that it is a mountain in Shinano. I think of that as I look at it. As I look at it, I think of the distance from here to Shinano.

---

◆　Season Word: *yukine*, "snowy peak." Winter, topography.

*Vocabulary:*
- *kano* is equivalent to modern *ano*, meaning "that over there" when referring to things distant from both the speaker and the listener.
- *kuni* in pre-modern times more often referred to a "province" than a "country/nation," so *Shinano no kuni* = "Shinano Province," the area of Nagano Prefecture today.
- *tōsa* is a noun form of *tōi* ("far/distant") → "distance/distantness." *Shinano no kuni no tōsa* = "the distance/distantness of Shinano Province."
- *mote* originally derives from *motsu* ("hold/carry") but functions like a particle meaning "[do] with/by means of." Here it implies a verb like *miru* ("look/gaze at"). *Tōsa mote miru* = "look/gaze at with (a sense of ) the distance/distantness."

すすみ来し　空間かへす　一螢火

*Susumi kishi*　　*kūkan kaesu*　　*ichi keika*

# A firefly's light
## returning in the same air
## within which it came.

Composed 1948.

A firefly lighted up and came toward me. The air was brightened by that light. Suddenly the firefly turned and went back in the direction from which he had come. The air he had flown in folded back on itself.

---

Season Word: *keika*, "firefly's light." Summer, animals.

*Vocabulary:*
- *susumi kishi* is a classical equivalent of *susunde kita*, the *-te* form of *susumu* ("advance/go forward") and the past form of *kuru* ("come"). A form of *kuru* after the *-te* form of a verb indicates the action moves in the direction of the speaker. *Susumi kishi* is a complete thought/sentence ("[he] came forward [toward me]") modifying *kūkan* ("air/space").
- *kaesu* means "turn over/fold back," and by extension, "return," so *kūkan (o) kaesu* means "folds back the space" as well as "returns through the space."
- *ichi* ("one") + *kei* ("firefly") + *ka* ("fire") = "the light of a single firefly."
- *susumi kishi kūkan kaesu* is a complete sentence ("folds back/returns through the space [he] came") that can be thought of either as ending in a colon or as modifying *ichi keika.*

小さきもの　　紙魚にも殖えて　　ともに遁ぐ
*Chisaki mono*　　*shimi ni mo fuete*　　*tomo ni nigu*

## *Tiny little things,*
## *even bookworms, multiply*
## *and flee together.*

Composed 1948.
Even bookworms have children in large numbers, and the children as
well as the parents eat paper. When people drive the parents away,
the children flee too. Their sins are small, but they flee too.

---

Season Word: *shimi*, "bookworm." Summer, animals.

*Vocabulary:*
- 紙魚 is literally "paper fish," an interesting coincidence with the English word "silverfish"; but the more familiar equivalent in English is "bookworm."
- *fuete* is the *-te* form of *fueru* ("increase/multiply," and, for animals, "propagate/breed").
- *nigu* is a classical equivalent of both 逃げる *nigeru* ("escape/run away") and 遁れる *nogareru* ("avoid/escape/seek refuge").

*Other points of interest:*
- the bookworm is every millimeter an insect nuisance in Japan. Readers of books that have been exposed to bookworms for a few years are familiar with the twisting tracks they leave behind in the pages.

翅触るる　まで雁のこゑ　かたまれり

*Hane fururu*　　*made kari no koe*　　*katamareri*

## *Voices of wild geese*
## *knotted so close together*
## *their wings make contact.*

Composed 1948.
A flock of geese passes over, in full cry. Their voices are so tightly combined, they must be extremely close together. Their wings may even be touching.

---

Season Word: *kari*, "wild geese." Autumn, animals.

*Vocabulary:*
- *fururu* is a classical equivalent of *fureru* ("touch").
- *made* = "until/to the extent of"
- こゑ is the old spelling of こえ *koe* ("voice," or, in the case of animals, "cry/song/call").
- *katamareri* is a classical equivalent of *katamatte-iru*, from *katamaru* ("lump/mass/crowd together").

111

蟷螂の　　眼の中までも　　枯れ尽す

Tōrō no　　me no naka made mo　　karetsukusu

# *Withering goes on*
# *even deep into the eyes*
# *of praying mantis.*

Composed 1948.

Winter has come, and a praying mantis has withered. His whole body has turned yellow. Even his eyes — even the centers of his eyes — are yellow. An entire yellowing! A complete withering!

Season Word: *tōrō*, "praying mantis." Autumn, animals.

*Vocabulary:*
- *tōrō no me no naka* is literally "the inside of the eyes of the praying mantis."
- *made* = "to/until" and *mo* is emphatic, so *made mo* = "even as far as/even unto."
- *kare* is from *kareru* ("wither") and *-tsukusu* as a verb suffix means "do completely/exhaustively/to the last," so *karetsukusu* means "wither completely."

舟漕いで　海の寒さの　中を行く
*Fune koide　　umi no samusa no　　naka o yuku*

*Pulling at his oars —*
*fisherman making his way*
*through the ocean's cold.*

Composed 1948.
A fisherman is rowing his boat into the offing to fish. I often hear from fishermen that it is cold out there. He is passing through the offing I think of as cold on his way to his fishing ground.

---

✦　Season Word: *samusa*, "the cold/coldness." Winter, season.

*Vocabulary:*
- *koide* is the *-te* form of *kogu* ("row/scull/paddle [a boat]"), here functioning essentially as an adverb for *yuku* (the alternate form of *iku*, "go").
- *samusa* is the noun form of *samui* ("cold"), so *umi no samusa no naka* is literally "inside/within the ocean's cold."
- the particle *o* means "through/along" when it connects a location word (*naka*) and a motion verb (*yuku*), so *naka o yuku* is "goes through" rather than "goes into."

# 海に鴨　　発砲直前　　かも知れず
Umi ni kamo　　happō chokuzen　　ka mo shirezu

## *Ducks on the ocean,*
## *in the time that goes before*
## *gunfire, I suppose.*

Composed 1949.
Ducks are floating on the ocean. Hunters are always after them, and only one shot kills. When I hear the shots, and I see the ducks on the ocean, I surmise that guns are being aimed at them.

---

Season Word: *kamo*, "ducks." Winter, animals.

*Vocabulary:*
- *happō* is a noun referring to the "firing/discharge/shot" of a gun, and *chokuzen* means "just before."
- *ka mo shirezu* is a classical equivalent of *ka mo shirenai*, an expression meaning "might/may be," so *happō chokuzen ka mo shirezu* = "might be just before the shot/gunfire."

巣を奪られ　　　たる親雀　　　天翔くる

*Su o torare* 　　　*-taru oyasuzume* 　　　*ama kakuru*

## *Robbed of their nestlings,*
## *the parent sparrows take wing*
## *into the heavens.*

Composed 1949.

The sparrows' nest has been robbed and the children taken. The parent sparrows have dashed into the sky and are flying about in the heavens. Their flight helps me to empathize with their inconsolable grief.

---

Season Word: *suzume no ko*, "sparrow nestling (implied)." Spring, animals.

*Vocabulary:*
- *toraretaru* is a classical equivalent of *torareta*, the passive past form of *toru* ("take"). When written with the kanji 奪, *toru* means "rob/steal." *Su o toraretaru* is a complete thought/sentence ("have been robbed of [their] nest") modifying *oyasuzume* ("parent ("sparrows"). The hyphen before *-taru* in the romanization shows that the poet is enjambing, or running two phrases together.
- *kakuru* is the classical form of *kakeru* ("soar/fly").

*Other points of interest:*
- the Japanese tree sparrow (*Passer montanus*) is the favorite bird of the Japanese, who enjoy watching the birds' domestic activities under the eaves of their homes. The birds are also anathema to farmers, since, after their nesting season is completed, they flock to the fields and ravage grain crops.

115

危ふきとき　蟹は土管に　入れば足る
*Ayauki toki*　*kani wa dokan ni*　*ireba taru*

# *In time of danger*
# *the crab only needs to go*
# *into a drainpipe.*

Composed 1949.

When danger approaches a crab, he runs and hides, like the crab I watched flee to safety in a drainpipe. A crab finds it simple to save his life.

---

Season Word: *kani*, "crab." Summer, animals.

*Vocabulary:*

- 危ふき is the classical *-ki* form of the adjective 危うい *ayaui* ("dangerous/hazardous/unsafe"). The *-ki* form is used when modifying nouns: *ayauki toki* = "dangerous time/time of danger."
- *ireba* is a classical equivalent of *haireba*, a conditional "if/when" form of *hairu* ("go into/come into/enter"). In classical Japanese, two separate *-ba* forms distinguish "if" and "when," and *ireba* can only mean "if [he] enters/goes into."
- *taru* is the classical form of *tariru* ("be enough/sufficient"), so *ireba taru* means "it is enough if he enters/goes into" → "all he needs to do is enter/go into."

116

一湾の　　潮しづもる　　きりぎりす

*Ichiwan no*　　*ushio shizumoru*　　*kirigirisu*

***Solitary bay***
***with the tide quieting down —***
***a cricket chirping.***

Composed 1949.

The tide had turned tranquil throughout Ise Bay. A cricket chirped in the grass near the water — the calm of the great tide; the faint voice of the cricket nearby.

---

◆　Season Word: *kirigirisu*, "cricket." Autumn, animals.

*Vocabulary:*
- *ichiwan* literally means "one bay" → "solitary bay." But using *ichi* ("one") as a prefix like this often implies "the whole/entire –," so *ichiwan no* implies "in/ throughout the whole bay."
- *ushio* = "tide/sea water."
- *shizumaru* means "turn quiet/calm/tranquil," while *shizumoru* means "the quiet/ calm/tranquility deepens."

117

虹の環を　　以て地上の　　ものかこむ
*Niji no wa o*　　　*motte chijō no*　　　*mono kakomu*

*In this rainbow's arch*
*all the things upon the earth*
*are now circumscribed.*

Composed 1950.
A rainbow describes a semicircle in the sky. Everything on earth is enclosed by it. To express it another way, the rainbow embraces everything on earth.

---

◆　Season Word: *niji*, "rainbow." Summer, celestial phenomena.

*Vocabulary:*
- *niji no wa* = "rainbow's ring/arch"
- . . . *o motte* following a noun means "with/by means of . . ." *Motte* is an alternate form of *mote*, seen in the poem on page 108.
- *o* has been omitted after *mono* ("things").
- *kakomu* = "encircle/surround."

118

虹を懸け　時が到れば　また外す

*Niji o kake*　　*toki ga itareba*　　*mata hazusu*

*He hung this rainbow,*
*and when the time comes again*
*He will take it down.*

Composed 1950.

A rainbow hung in the sky, but after a time it disappeared. If there was a rainbow in the sky, someone hung it there. And if it disappeared, he took it away. All the things of the heavens are God's work.

---

Season Word: *niji,* "rainbow." Summer, celestial phenomena.

*Vocabulary:*
- *kake* is essentially an abbreviated *-te* form of *kakeru* ("hang up/suspend"); *niji o kake(te)* = "hang a rainbow, and . . ."
- *itareba* is a conditional form of *itaru* ("reach/arrive at"), and *toki ga itareba* means "when the time comes."
- strictly speaking, *mata* modifies *hazusu* ("remove/take off"): *mata hazusu* = "takes [it] off again."

119

瓜貰ふ　　太陽の熱　　さめざるを
*Uri morau*　　*taiyō no netsu*　　*samezaru o*

# *Given a melon*
## *with all the heat of the sun*
### *still warm within it.*

Composed 1950.

I passed a melon field when the farm family was out there, and they gave me a melon. The melon I took into my hands had the original heat of the sun. I got it straight from the field.

---

Season Word: *uri*, "melon." Summer, plants.

*Vocabulary:*
- 貰ふ is the old spelling of 貰う *morau* ("receive").
- *samezaru* is a classical equivalent of *samenai*, the negative form of *sameru* ("cool down/get cold.")
- in classical Japanese, the particle *o* at the end of a sentence is exclamatory.

噴水　高揚る　水玉が　水玉追ひ

*Funsui*　*takaagaru*　*mizutama ga*　*mizutama oi*

*Fountain spray rising;*
*drops of water going up,*
*others following.*

Composed 1950.
A fountain is spraying water into the air. At its highest point each drop of water is clearly visible. Drops of water go up, and drops of water follow them. The drops of water play Follow the Leader. The meter is an irregular 4, 5, 5, 6.

---

◆　Season Word: *funsui*, "fountain." Summer, life.

*Vocabulary:*
- *takaagaru* = "climb/rise up high" (see page 76).
- 追ひ is the old spelling of 追い *oi*, the stem form of 追う *ou* ("chase/pursue/follow after"). Here the stem form of *ou* functions essentially like the *-te* form, *otte*, indicating, by inverted syntax, how/in what manner the fountain is rising/spraying up. Normal order would be *mizutama ga mizutama (o) oi (= otte) funsui takaagaru*: literally, "With water drop chasing water drop, the fountain sprays up high."

三方壁　そこへ入り来し　碧揚羽

*Sanbō kabe*　　*soko e iri kishi*　　*ao-ageha*

# *A U-shaped alley —*
# *making his way into it,*
# *a blue swallowtail.*

Composed 1951.

A cul-de-sac formed by three walls, into which a beautiful blue swallowtail butterfly enters. Having nowhere to go, she flutters in confusion. Those walls have driven the butterfly into a corner.

---

Season Word: *ao-ageha*, "blue swallowtail." Spring, animals.

*Vocabulary:*
- *sanbō* literally means "three directions" and *kabe* means "wall(s)," so *sanbō kabe* means "walls in three directions."
- *iri kishi* is a classical equivalent of *haitte kita*, the *-te* form of *hairu* ("go in/come in/enter") and the past form of *kuru* ("come") → "came in."
- *soko e iri kishi* is a complete thought/sentence ("came into there/that place") modifying *ao ageha* ("blue swallowtail").

# 手を入れて　井の噴き上ぐる　ものに触る

*Te o irete*　　　*i no fukiaguru*　　　*mono ni furu*

## I thrust my hand in
## and feel something driving up
## out of the well's depths.

Composed 1951.

It is a well, with water being driven with great force out of its depths.
I thrust my hand into the well and feel the water rising upward. How
pleasant it is to feel the power of rising water.

---

✦　Season Word: *i no fuki*, "spurting of a well." Summer, topography.

*Vocabulary:*
- *irete* is the *-te* form of *ireru* ("put in/insert").
- 噴井 *fuki-i*, implied by the poem and referred to explicitly in the author's note, is an "artesian well."
- *fukiaguru* is a classical equivalent of *fukiageru* ("blow/spray/spurt up" → "drive up"), from *fuku* ("blow/emit") and *ageru* ("lift/raise up"). *Fukiaguru* modifies *mono* ("thing"): "the thing/force that drives up."
- *furu* is the classical form of *fureru* ("touch/feel").

123

雪積みし　　ところより海　　更に退く
*Yuki tsumishi*　　*tokoro yori umi*　　*sara-ni hiku*

## *Ocean backing off*
## *ever further from the place*
## *where the snow remains.*

Composed 1952

Snow has piled up white on the ocean shore. The ocean once bordered on that white stretch of beach, but now, with the tide receded, it is far away. Now there is the white beach, a wet shoreline, and the ocean.

---

Season Word: *yuki*, "snow." Winter, celestial phenomena.

*Vocabulary:*
- *tsumishi* is a classical equivalent of *tsumotta*, the past form of *tsumoru* ("pile up"). *Yuki tsumishi* is a complete thought/sentence ("snow has piled up") modifying *tokoro* ("place").
- *yori* = "from."
- *sara-ni* = "once again/even more/more and more."
- *hiku* = "retreat/recede."

沖までの　　途中に春の　　月懸る
*Oki made no*　　*tochū ni haru no*　　*tsuki kakaru*

# *The spring moon hanging*
## *in the sky halfway from here*
### *to the open sea.*

Composed 1952.
When I look at the ocean from the shore, I see the spring moon. The offing appears to lie far beyond the moon. The spring moon hangs halfway between here and the open sea, and bends toward me.

---

Season Word: *haru no tsuki*, "spring moon." Spring, celestial phenomena.

*Vocabulary:*
- *oki* = "the offing" and *oki made* = "up to/as far as the offing," but *. . . no tochū* means "on the way to/part way to . . . ," so *oki made no tochū* means "part way to the offing."
- *kakaru* = "hang/be suspended (from/in)."

籠を出て　一翔長き　螢火よ

*Kago o dete　　isshō nagaki　　hotarubi yo*

# *The protracted glow*
# *of the fleeing firefly*
# *once out of the cage!*

Composed 1952.

A firefly flies from a cage. The firefly's light goes on and continues burning for a great distance. It is a desperate flight, occasioned by his release from human hands. It is a flame of joy.

---

Season Word: *hotaru*, "firefly." Summer, animals.

*Vocabulary:*
- *dete* is the *-te* form of *deru* ("go/come out/exit/leave").
- 翔 *shō* means "fly/soar," and the prefix *is-* (for *ichi*, "one") makes it "one flight."
- *nagaki* is the classical *-ki* form of the adjective *nagai* ("long"). *Isshō nagaki* modifies *hotarubi* ("firefly light"): "firefly light in one long flight."
- *yo* is an exclamatory particle.

氷を提ぐ　透明なれど　重きらし

*Kōri o sagu*　*tōmei naredo*　*omoki rashi*

*Ice being carried —*
*although it is transparent,*
*it still looks heavy.*

Composed 1952.
The iceman comes in carrying ice. It is transparent ice, for the icebox. It
is so transparent it looks weightless. The iceman acts as if it is heavy.

---

Season Word: *natsu no kōri*, "summer ice" (implied). Summer, life.

*Vocabulary:*
- *sagu* is the classical form of *sageru* ("carry at one's side [like a pail]"), but in this
  case is equivalent to its progressive form, *sagete-iru* ("[is] carrying").
- *tōmei* = "transparent."
- *naredo* is a classical form meaning "although it is . . ."
- *omoki* is the classical *-ki* form of the adjective *omoi* ("heavy").
- *rashi* is the old form of *rashii*, "appears/seems to be." An adjective must be in the
  *-ki* form when followed by *rashi*.

127

ダイヴィング　空中のこと　短きかな
*Daivingu*　　　　　*kūchū no koto*　　　*mijikaki kana*

*Diver in the air —*
*how little time goes by before*
*he hits the water!*

Composed 1953.

A diver stands on a diving platform, then he pushes off the platform and dives into the pool. The time between the platform and the pool is very short — the time it takes a man to fall.

---

Season Word: *daivingu*, "diving." Summer, life.

*Vocabulary:*
- since Japanese lacks a *v* sound, the common practice has been to convert it to *b* (バ*ba*, ビ*bi*, ブ*bu*, ベ*be*, ボ*bo*, ) in katakana renderings of foreign loan words, but some writers use ヴ as the katakana equivalent of *v* (or, strictly speaking, *vu*): ヴァ*va*, ヴィ*vi*, ヴ*vu*, ヴェ*ve*, ヴォ*vo*. Each is pronounced as a single syllable even if written with two kana.
- *kūchū* is literally "air/sky" + "middle/inside." *Koto* means "thing" in an abstract sense, referring variously to "circumstance/event/occasion/experience/etc.," so *kūchū no koto* can be thought of as "the time in the air."
- *mijikaki* is the classical *-ki* form of *mijikai* ("short/brief").
- *kana* is a classical exclamatory particle.

128

人を容れし　　幕営の幕　　畳まるる
*Hito o ireshi*　　*bakuei no baku*　　*tatamaruru*

# *Folded is the tent*
# *that during the camping trip*
# *surrounded people.*

Composed 1953.
A camp tent: people can fit in it; people can sleep in it. When day breaks,
it is taken down, flattened, and made into a small package. The cloth that
held people is flattened into baggage.

---

Season Word: *kyanpingu*, "camping" (implied). Summer, life.

*Vocabulary:*
- *ireshi* is a classical equivalent of *ireta*, the past form of *ireru* ("put/let in"); the past form can mean "contained/held in," and this meaning is reinforced here by the kanji 容, one of whose meanings is "content." *Hito o ireshi* ("[it] contained people") and *bakuei* ("camp/camping") separately modify *baku* ("curtain/draped fabric/tent").
- *tatamaruru* is a classical equivalent of *tatamareta*, the past form of *tatamareru* ("be folded"): "was/has been folded" → "is folded (up)."

腐に金蠅　　いまのいままで　　いづこにゐし

*Fu ni kinbae*　　*ima no ima made*　　*izuko ni ishi*

*These green bottle flies*
*on carrion here — where on earth*
*were they until now?*

Composed 1953.
Green bottle flies have gathered on something rotten. It is natural that
they should gather there, but it was so sudden! Where were they;
where did they come from?

---

Season Word: *hae* (changed to *bae* for euphony), "fly." Summer, animals.

*Vocabulary:*
- *fu* means "rot/decay" but is here being used as a noun, "something rotting/decaying."
- *ima* = "now" and *made* = "until"; *ima no ima made* is an expression meaning "until just now/until this very moment."
- *izuko* is an archaic word for "where." This word makes the poem a question even without the usual question particle *ka* at the end.
- ゐし *ishi* is a classical equivalent of いた *ita*, past form of *iru* ("be/exist"). ゐ belonged to the *wa* column of the syllabary, but has now fallen out of use and been replaced by い.

幾十年　使ひ来し身の　露に濡れ

*Ikujūnen    tsukai kishi mi no    tsuyu ni nure*

***This corporal frame***
***that I have used for decades***
***is now wet with dew.***

Composed 1953.

I am wet with the dew of a path I took through the fields. This body wet with dew is a body I have used for many decades. Now it is wet with dew — an extraordinary dew.

---

Season Word: *tsuyu,* "dew." Autumn, celestial phenomena.

*Vocabulary:*
- *iku* = "how many," *jū* = "ten," and *nen* = "year," so *ikujūnen* is literally "how many tens of years" → "how many decades?" In certain contexts, as here, it simply means "several/many decades."
- *tsukai kishi* is equivalent to modern *tsukatte kita*, the *-te* form of *tsukau* ("use") and the past form of *kuru* ("come"). One of the meanings of *kuru/kita* after the *-te* form of a verb is that the action has occurred continuously/continually down to the present.
- *ikujūnen tsukai kishi* is a complete thought/sentence ("used for many decades") modifying *mi* ("body"). *No* in this case is equivalent to *ga*, marking *mi* as the subject of *nure* ("become wet").

131

大和また　新たなる国　田を鋤けば

*Yamato mata　aratanaru kuni　ta o sukeba*

## *Dig up its rice fields*
## *and the land of Yamato*
## *becomes new again.*

Composed 1954.

Yamato is an old land. When I went there in the spring, they were tilling the fields. The turned, tilled soil was new. The old land was dug, the new earth appeared, and the land became new. Year by year, age by age.

---

✦ Season Word: *ta suki*, "plowing ricefields." Spring, life.

*Vocabulary:*
- *aratanaru* = "new/renewed."
- *sukeba* is a conditional ("when") form of *suku* ("plow/turn over soil"). The poem is in inverted syntax. Normal order would be *Ta o sukeba, Yamato mata aratanaru kuni*, with something like *da/desu* ("is") implied at the end.

*Other points of interest:*
- Yamato was the area around present-day Nara where the first unified state of Japan arose during the 4th through 8th centuries, and the word is used broadly as the aboriginal name for Japan. From 710 to 784, the city of Nara was the nation's first "permanent" capital in the lavish Chinese mode.

谷へ汚水　今年あと　幾許もなし

*Tani e osui*　*kotoshi ato*　*ikubaku mo nashi*

***Raw sewage flowing***
***into the valley; not much***
***left in the old year.***

Composed 1954.
Just before midnight on the last day of the year, I threw dirty water
into the valley from my valley dwelling. The sound was the sound of
washing out the detritus of the old year. The year would end soon.

---

Season Word: (去年)今年 *(kozo) kotoshi*, "last year, this year" (implied). New Year's, life.

*Vocabulary:*
- *ato* before a quantity means "(that much/many) remaining."
- *ikubaku* can mean either "how much" or "a certain sum," but the expression *ikubaku mo nai* means "(there is) hardly any at all." *Nashi* is the classical "dictionary form" of *nai* ("is none/have none").

落花とぶ　時の外には　生きられず

*Rakka tobu　　toki no soto ni wa　　ikirarezu*

## *Blossoms in the air —*
## *unable to stay longer*
## *and still escape time.*

Composed 1955.
Cherry blossoms are flying through the air. Their movement is controlled by time. This is true not only of plants, but of human beings too. We cannot escape the world of time.

---

Season Word: *rakka*, "(falling) blossoms." Spring, plants.

*Vocabulary:*
- *rakka tobu*, literally "falling flowers fly," is a complete sentence with a full stop. *Toki* ("time") begins a second sentence, but the implied subject remains *rakka*.
- *toki no soto* is literally "outside of time."
- *ikirarezu* is equivalent to *ikirarenai*, the negative potential form ("cannot –") of *ikiru* ("live/exist") → "[the falling flowers] cannot live/exist [outside of time]."

この床几　吾も休めど　遍路のもの

*Kono shōgi*　　*ware mo yasumedo*　　*henro no mono*

***Although I sit here
on this travel stool awhile,
it is for pilgrims.***

Composed 1955.
A stool had been set out along the pilgrimage road through Shikoku.
Without any ado, I sat down on it. Properly speaking, it was for
pilgrims. I was just borrowing it for a short rest.

---

Season Word: *henro*, "pilgrimage." Spring, observances.

*Vocabulary:*
- *ware* means "I/me" in classical Japanese; *ware mo* = "I, too, . . ."
- *yasumedo* = "although I rest," from *yasumu* ("rest").
- *henro* can be either "pilgrimage" or "pilgrim."
- *no* is possessive, so *henro no mono* literally means "the pilgrims' thing" →
  "belongs to/is for the pilgrims."

渦潮を　　　両国の岬　　　立ちて見る
*Uzushio o*　　　*futaguni no saki*　　　*tachite miru*

## *The promontories*
## *of two provinces standing*
## *watching the maelstrom.*

Composed 1956.
The straits of Naruto are very narrow between Monzaki, in Awaji,
and Magozaki, in Tokushima. The rising and falling of the sea create
a whirlpool. The high promontories of Monzaki and Magozaki
overlook the maelstrom.

---

✦　Season Word: *uzushio*, "whirlpool." Spring, topography.

*Vocabulary:*
- *futa* is "two" in traditional Japanese counting, but using the kanji 両 also implies "both (of a pair)." *Kuni* changes to *guni* for euphony and in this case means "province/prefecture" rather than "country/nation."
- 岬 *saki*, more commonly read *misaki*, means "cape/promontory/headland."
- *tachite* is the old *-te* form of *tatsu* ("stand"). *Tachite miru* = "stand and look/watch."

渦潮を　　落ちゆく船の　　姿して
*Uzushio o*　　*ochi yuku fune no*　　*sugata shite*


*Into the whirlpool,*
*a ship descending, holding*
*the shape of a ship.*


Composed 1956.
As I looked down on the whirlpool from Monzaki, a steamer passed
through on its way from the Inland Sea into the Pacific. She was
tossed about like an object in a maelstrom, but viewed from the rear
as she headed into the Pacific she was undeniably a ship.

---

Season Word: *uzushio*, "whirlpool." Spring, topography.

*Vocabulary:*
- *ochi yuku* means "go falling down into." *Uzushio o ochi yuku* ("go falling down into a whirlpool") can modify *fune* ("ship") for the meaning, "a ship falling down into a whirlpool." *Ochi yuku* can also have a second meaning here: "(a ship) descends (through the whirlpools), and proceeds onward."
- *sugata shite* is the *-te* form of *sugata (o) suru*, "have/take on a look/appearance," or, as a modifier, "with the appearance/look of."
- the poem essentially needs to be read twice: "Looking like a ship (that might) go falling down into a whirlpool, the ship descends (the current) through the whirlpools and sails off, (surviving the trip and) still looking very much like a ship."

遅れ咲き　いまの落花に　加はらず

*Okure saki*　　　*ima no rakka ni*　　　*kuwawarazu*

## *Late blooming cherries —*
## *contributing no petals*
## *to those falling now.*

Composed 1956.

The petals of the early blossoming cherries have begun to fall. Not one petal of the late-blooming ones has fallen. There is a definite boundary between the two.

Season Word: *rakka*, "(falling) blossoms." Spring, plants.

*Vocabulary:*
- *okure* (from *okureru*, "be late") + *saki* (from *saku*, "bloom") here is an abbreviation of something like *okurete saita sakura*, "cherries that bloomed late" → "late-blooming cherries."
- 加はらず *kuwawarazu* is the old spelling of 加わらず, the negative form of *kuwawaru* ("join").

手に挟み　　牡丹の面を　　まざと見る

*Te ni hasami*　　*botan no omo o*　　*maza-to miru*

*Peony blossom —*
*I clutch it between my hands*
*and stare in its face.*

Composed 1956.
I looked at a peony, a great-blossomed peony. I approached it,
cupped its face in my hands, and gazed at it. It was a beautiful face. I
gazed at its face endlessly.

---

Season Word: *botan*, "peony." Summer, plants.

*Vocabulary:*
- *hasami* is from *hasamu* ("hold/sandwich between"); *hasami* here acts like the *-te*
  form: *hasande . . . miru* → "hold between [my hands] and look."
- *omo* ("face/surface") has now mostly been replaced by the word *omote*.
- *maza-to* is an adverb implying either that an image appears "vividly/clearly," or
  that one is looking intently at something in order to gain a vivid/clear picture.

太陽の　出でて没るまで　青岬

*Taiyō no*　　　*idete iru made*　　　*aomisaki*

**A cape always green,**
**from the time the sun comes up**
**until it goes down.**

Composed 1956.

Shiono-misaki is covered with green grass. When the sun comes up, it is already green. As the sun rides across the sky, it continues green, and it is still green when the sun sets in the west — an ever-green cape.

---

◆　Season Word: *aomisaki,* "green cape." Summer, topography.

*Vocabulary:*
- *no* is equivalent to *ga,* marking the subject of the verbs, *idete* and *iru.*
- *idete* is the *-te* form of the classical equivalent of *deru* ("come out/go out/ emerge").
- *iru* means "go/goes into," or, when speaking of the sun, "sets."
- *made* after a verb means "until" that action/event takes place.
- whether *ao* means "blue" or "green" must be determined by context.

歓びの　　時は過ぎゆく　　鵜川迅し
*Yorokobi no*　　*toki wa sugi yuku*　　*ugawa hayashi*

*Cormorants' river —*
*all the rapture of that time,*
*gone with the rapids.*

Composed 1956.
I watched the cormorant-fishing and found it interesting and enjoyable. Yet the joy of the time passed quickly. The swift water of the river the cormorants fished swept away those moments of rapture.

Season Word: *ugawa*, "cormorant stream." Summer, life.

*Vocabulary:*
- *sugi* is from *sugiru* ("pass/go by") and *yuku* is an alternate form of *iku* ("go"), so *sugi yuku* is like saying "goes passing by." This phrase applies both to *toki* ("time") and to *ugawa* ("cormorant stream/river").
- *hayashi* is the classical form of *hayai* ("[is] fast/swift").

*Other points of interest:*
- cormorant fishing is a popular tourist attraction, particularly along Nagara River in Gifu Prefecture. The birds are tethered and fitted with collars and thus cannot swallow the fish their handlers encourage them to catch. They work at night, off boats lighted by blazing torches.

鵜の川の　　迅さよ時の　　流れより
*U no kawa no*　*hayasa yo toki no*　*nagare yori*

## *How swift the water*
## *of the cormorants' river —*
## *swifter than the hours.*

Composed 1956.
The waters which the cormorants fish are very swift. They slip by
with great speed. Surely those waters are under the control of time,
but they are even faster than the ticking of time.

---

✦　Season Word: *u no kawa*, "cormorant stream." Summer, life.

*Vocabulary:*
- *hayasa* is the noun form of *hayai* ("fast/swift"), and *yo* is exclamatory, so *hayasa yo* is like "Oh, the speed [of the river]!"
- *toki no nagare* = "the flow of time"
- . . . *yori* means "more than . . ." — in this case implying "faster than . . ."

鵜篝の　　　早瀬を過ぐる　　　大炎上
*Ukagari no*　　　*hayase o suguru*　　　*daienjō*

## *The great burst of flame*
## *as cormorant torch passes*
## *over rough water!*

Composed 1956.
Cormorant fishing on Nagara River. I was permitted to ride down the river with the birds, wearing black clothing. As we rode the swift currents, the torch burned brightly, in a great conflagration. It was the supreme experience of cormorant fishing.

---

◆　Season Word: *ukagari*, "cormorant torch." Summer, life.

*Vocabulary:*
- *no* can be thought of both as an equivalent to *ga*, marking the subject (*ukagari ga . . . suguru* = "cormorant torches pass"), and as the particle for modifying one noun with another (*ukagari no . . . daienjō* = "the great conflagration of cormorant torches").
- *suguru* is the old form of *sugiru* ("pass/go by/go through"). (*Ukagari no*) *hayase o suguru* is a complete thought/sentence ("[cormorant torch] passes through/over the rapids") that can be read both as a modifier for *daienjō*, and as an independent clause ending in a colon.

143

曝涼に　　けふは昇殿　　地を見下す

*Bakuryō ni*　　*kyō wa shōden*　　*chi o miorosu*

## *Day for airing out —*
## *I stand in an august place*
## *and survey the ground.*

Composed 1956.
They air out the Imperial treasures of the Shōsōin in autumn. I was
allowed to witness it, and climbed the temporary staircase to the
treasure house built of squared logs. I could see the ground below
me, as I stood in an honored place and looked down from that height.

---

Season Word: *Shōsōin bakuryō*, "Shōsōin airing out." Autumn, observances.

*Vocabulary:*
- *bakuryō* ("airing") is made up of kanji that mean "expose (to air/sun)" and "cool/ refreshing." *Bakuryō ni* = "for the airing."
- けふ is the old spelling for きょう *kyō* ("today").

*Other points of interest:*
- the Shōsōin in Nara is one of the great repositories of historical treasures, many of which are, like the original wooden building, well over a thousand years old (for safety, the treasures are now housed in two separate ferroconcrete buildings). The Shōsōin is never open to the public but goes through a great airing once a year. Seishi's invitation to be present there at such a time was a great honor.

冬山に　ピッケル突きて　抜きしあと
*Fuyuyama ni*　*pikkeru tsukite*　*nukishi ato*

*A winter mountain —*
*the tracks made by an ice-axe,*
*pushed in and pulled out.*

Composed 1956.
When I say "winter mountain," I mean a snow-covered mountain.
Sharp holes had been punched in the snow of the road. When I
looked at them, I knew they had been made by an ice-axe, driven in
and quickly pulled out again.

---

Season Word: *fuyuyama*, "winter mountain." Winter, topography.

*Vocabulary:*
- *pikkeru* is a katakana rendering of German *Pickel*, meaning "ice axe."
- *tsukite* is the old *-te* form of *tsuku* ("poke/stab").
- *nukishi* is a classical equivalent of *nuita*, the past form of *nuku* ("pull out/withdraw").
- *ato* refers to the "mark/track" left behind by something. *Pikkeru tsukite nukishi* is a complete thought/sentence ("drove in an ice axe and drew it back out") modifying *ato*.

145

大露頭　　　赭くてそこは　　雪積まず

*Dairotō*　　　*akakute soko wa*　　*yuki tsumazu*

*A broad vein of ore,*
*       copper-colored in one place*
*     where no snow remains.*

Composed 1957.

I went to the top of the copper mine in Besshi. It was covered with snow, except for a spot in the middle where the ground was red. It was a broad vein of copper. Because of the miasma of copper, the snow had not stayed.

---

◆　Season Word: *yuki*, "snow." Winter, celestial phenomena.

*Vocabulary:*
- *dai* is a prefix for kanji compounds meaning "large/great," and *rotō* is literally "exposed head" → "outcrop."
- *akakute* is the *-te* form of the adjective *akai* ("red"). The kanji 赭 is used specifically for earth/ore that is red in color.
- *tsumazu* is the classical negative form of *tsumu* ("pile up/accumulate"), so *yuki tsumazu* is literally "snow does not accumulate."

146

海上の　　見知らぬ村は　　烏賊火村

*Kaijō no*　　*mishiranu mura wa*　　*ikabimura*

# *Out on the ocean,*
# *an unfamiliar village —*
# *village of squid lights.*

Composed 1958.

Out on the sea is a lighted village. The lights aren't there all the time, they are the lamps of squid-fishing boats, standing in a row. The lights belong to the place called Squid-light Town.

---

Season Word: *ika*, "squid." Summer, animals.

*Vocabulary:*

- *mishiranu* = "unknown/unfamiliar."
- *ika* = "squid" and *-bi* = "fires/lights" (from *hi*, with the *h* changing to *b* for euphony).
- *mura* means "village." The formal name of any small community officially classed as a "village" ends in *-mura*, so *ikabimura* not only describes the village but also sounds like the proper name of the village.

147

南北の　　夜の通風に　　祇園囃子
*Nanboku no　　yo no tsūfū ni　　Gion-bayashi*

*The wind carries it*
*through the night, from north to south —*
*the Gion music.*

Composed 1958.
In Kyōto, I heard the music of the Gion Festival. The wind from north
to south carried the music through the city streets.

---

Season Word: *Gion-bayashi*, "Gion music." Summer, observances.

*Vocabulary:*
- *tsūfū* is "air that circulates/wind that blows by."
- *ni* in this case means "on," implying "carried on [the wind]."

*Other points of interest:*
- the Gion festival is celebrated in various parts of Japan and is connected with the service for the dead celebrated at India's Jetavana monastery — or *Gion Shōja*, as the Japanese call it. The best known Gion festival takes place in the neighborhood of the Yasaka Shrine, in Kyōto.

施餓鬼川　水晶の数珠　ばらけ散る
Segakigawa　　suishō no juzu　　barake chiru

## *Mass on the river —*
## *crystals of the rosary*
## *scatter in the water.*

Composed 1958.
I was in a boat, attending a mass for the dead. The priest rubbed the crystal rosary violently. Suddenly the rosary broke apart and scattered its crystals in the muddy river — those transparent crystals!

Season Word: *kawa segaki*, "service for the dead by drowning in rivers." Autumn, observances.

*Vocabulary:*
- *segaki* refers to a ritual performed in memory of the unmourned dead. When performed on water, it is in memory of those who have died of drowning. *Segakigawa* (from *kawa*, "river") can be any river on which such a ritual is being performed.
- *suishō no juzu* = "crystal rosary."
- *barake* (from *barakeru*) and *chiru* both mean "scatter/disperse."

149

冬河に　　新聞全紙　　浸り浮く
*Fuyukawa ni　　shinbun zenshi　　tsukari uku*

*A wintry river,*

*with a newspaper open*

*wide on the water.*

Composed 1958.
The Ibi River, in Kuwana — a big river, even in winter. I looked at it from the Funatsuya Inn and saw something rectangular floating on it. It was a wide open newspaper — a full two-page spread floating on the great wintry river.

---

Season Word: *fuyukawa*, "wintry river." Winter, topography.

*Vocabulary:*
- *shinbun* = "newspaper."
- *zenshi*, combining the kanji for "all/complete" and "paper," can mean "the full/whole newspaper" or "all newspapers," but here, as the author's note clarifies, it means "a full sheet from a newspaper."
- *tsukari* is from *tsukaru* ("bathe in/be immersed in/be soaked in"), and *uku* means "float(s)."

寒風の　砂丘今日見る　今日のかたち

*Kanpū no*　　*sakyū kyō miru*　　　*kyō no katachi*

***Dunes in a cold wind —***
***the shape they take before me,***
***the shape of today.***

Composed 1959.
I went to the dunes in Tottori in the middle of the winter. A cold
wind was blowing fiercely, making the sand fly, changing the shape
of the dunes constantly. I took in the shape the dunes held at that
moment.

---

Season Word: *kanpū*, "cold wind." Winter, celestial phenomena.

*Vocabulary:*
- *kanpū no sakyū* = "dunes in a/the cold wind."
- *kyō* = today and *kyō miru* = "I look at [them] today."
- *kyō no katachi* = "today's shape/[their] shape today."

燈台は　　　光の館　　　桜の夜
*Tōdai wa*　　*hikari no yakata*　　*sakura no yo*

# The beacon chamber
# is the dwelling place of light —
# cherry blossom night.

Composed 1959.

I went to the lighthouse on Hino Point, in Wakayama. The chamber of the lighthouse was lighted, making the lighthouse a house of light. Under it a cherry tree was in bloom, but it was dark. It was a cherry blossom night, but the lighthouse alone was the house of light.

---

Season Word: *sakura*, "cherry blossoms." Spring, plants.

*Vocabulary:*
- *tōdai* = "lighthouse."
- *hikari* = "light."
- *yakata* refers to the dwellings of high-placed persons, such as nobility and feudal lords: "castle/palace/mansion." *Hikari no yakata* is like saying "palace of light/ dwelling place of light."

152

虎杖は　　城塁の花　　石の花
Itadori wa　　jōrui no hana　　ishi no hana

## *Japanese knotweed —*
## *the flower of castle walls,*
## *the flower of stone.*

Composed 1959.

Between the stones of a castle wall, a Japanese knotweed grows, and blossoms. The flower blooms with the aid of the castle wall, with the aid of the stone wall. If the knotweed heard me calling its flower "the stone flower," it would surely respond, "That's exactly right."

---

Season Word: *itadori (no hana)*, "Japanese knotweed flower." Summer, plants.

*Vocabulary:*
* *jōrui* can refer either to the castle/fortress as a whole or more specifically to the castle wall/enclosure.
* *no* = "of."

雪掻きて　雪嶺に白き　道つくる
*Yuki kakite*　*yukine ni shiroki*　*michi tsukuru*

*Shoveling the snow*
*away from a snowy peak,*
*making a white road.*

Composed 1959.
The summit of Mount Gozaisho, in the Suzuka Mountains. Snow had accumulated on the mountain, and the ropeway people were clearing it away. Even after the snow was cleared, the dirt of the road remained hidden. It was a snow road, a white road.

---

Season Word: *yuki*, "snow." Winter, celestial phenomena.

*Vocabulary:*
- the particle *o*, marking the direct object, has been omitted after *yuki*.
- *kakite* is the old *-te* form of *kaku*, meaning "scratch/scrape," or, when speaking of snow, "shovel/clear away."
- 嶺, by itself read *mine*, means "peak/summit"; *yukine* = "snow-covered peak."
- *shiroki* is the classical *-ki* form, for modifying nouns, of the adjective *shiroi* ("white").
- a *rōpu-uē*, from English "ropeway," is the standard Japanese term for an aerial tramway/railway that runs under overhead cables.

154

雪嶺の　　　大三角を　　　鎌と呼ぶ
*Setsurei no*　　*daisankaku o*　　*Kama to yobu*

## *The great triangle*
## *that is this snowy mountain*
## *they call, "The Sickle."*

Composed 1959.
Mount Gozaisho and Mount Kama, in the Suzuka Mountains. When
one stands on snowy Gozaisho, Mount Kama across the valley
describes a great triangle of snow. The local people affectionately
call it "The Sickle."

---

✦　Season Word: *setsurei*, "snowy peak." Winter, topography.

*Vocabulary:*
- the kanji compound 雪嶺 is here given the *on* reading (*setsurei*) derived from the original Chinese sounds for the kanji, while it was given the native Japanese *kun* reading (*yukine*) in the previous poem. The meaning does not change.
- *sankaku* = "triangle," and *daisankaku* = "great triangle."
- *kama* = "sickle," so the name Mount Kama literally means "Mount Sickle."
- *to* indicates a quote, so . . . *to yobu* = "[they] call it . . ."

*Other points of interest:*
- the sickle is an important tool for Japanese farmers. It is a rugged tool, with a straight handle fastened at a right angle to a sharp, nearly straight blade.

修二会見る　　棧女人の眼　　女人の眼
*Shunie miru*　　　*san nyonin no me*　　*nyonin no me*

*Water-drawing rite —*
*women's eyes through the lattice,*
*women's eyes watching.*

Composed 1960.
Women who watch the water-drawing ceremony must stand behind a lattice-work barrier. I sat in the sanctuary, and when I looked at the barrier, I saw women's eyes in every opening — eyes filled with the sadness of being denied entrance to the sanctuary.

---

Season Word: *shunie*, "water-drawing rite." Spring, observances.

*Vocabulary:*
- *san* is a "grating/lattice" used as a partition.
- 女人 *nyonin* is a kanji compound literally meaning "female person(s)." *Nyonin no me* = "women's eyes."

*Other points of interest:*
- strictly speaking, the *o-mizu-tori* ("water-drawing ceremony") is only a single part of the *shunie* (or *shunigatsue*) rites, which are held over a two-week period in early March at the Tōdaiji temple in Nara. *O-mizu-tori* has become a common name for the entire *shunie* because it is performed at the climax of the rites.

万緑に　　薬石板を　　打ち減らす
*Banryoku ni*　　*yakusekiban o*　　*uchi herasu*

# Temple striking-board,
### grown thinner from the pounding
### of green-leaves season.

Composed 1960.
A striking board hung in one of the halls of Eihei-ji Temple, its wood worn from being beaten to announce meal after meal. During the green-leaves season, the striking board takes a battering.

---

◆　Season Word: *banryoku*, "green-leaves season." Summer, plants.

*Vocabulary:*
- 万 *ban* or *man* is familiar as meaning "ten thousand," but it is also often used to mean "all/everything." 緑 *ryoku*, usually read *midori* by itself, means "green," so *banryoku* literally means "all things are green." The word often refers to the season when all things are green.
- *yakuseki*, literally "medicine stone," originally referred to the heated stone Zen monks used to overcome feelings of hunger and cold from not having an evening meal. Later, however, *yakuseki* came to mean "evening meal." Since *-ban* means "board," *yakusekiban* is literally "evening meal board," or just "meal board."
- *uchi* is from *utsu*, "hit/strike/pound," and *herasu* means "reduce/decrease/lessen," so *uchi herasu* means "reduce/wear away by pounding."

ナイターに　見る夜の土　不思議な土
*Naitā ni　　miru yoru no tsuchi　fushigi-na tsuchi*

### *Mysterious ground —*
### *the ground I watch in the night*
### *of a night-ballgame.*

Composed 1960.
I was in for a surprise when I saw a night baseball game for the first
time. The field was brilliantly lighted from three directions, making
the ground look so mysterious as to be not of this world.

---

Season Word: *naitā*, "night baseball game." Summer, life.

*Vocabulary:*
- *naitā* ("nighter"), a word invented by the Japanese to refer to a night baseball
  game, is frequently cited as an example of the Japanese penchant for creating
  new words by adapting foreign words. When the word "nighter" is now occasion-
  ally used in English, it is in fact a loan word from Japanese.
- *naitā ni miru* is a complete thought/sentence ("[I] see/saw [it] at a night game")
  modifying *yoru no tsuchi* ("earth/ground at night").
- *fushigi-na* = "wonderful/marvelous/mysterious/indescribable."

158

奈良の月　山出て寺の　上に来る

*Nara no tsuki　yama dete tera no　ue ni kuru*

## The moon at Nara,
## rising above the temple
## out of the mountains.

Composed 1960.

I was present at a moon-viewing party at Tōshōdai-ji Temple. The harvest moon emerged from behind the Nara mountains, crossed the sky and made its way to above the Tōshōdai-ji. The time it took to come from the mountain to the temple.

---

Season Word: *tsuki*, "moon." Autumn, celestial phenomena.

*Vocabulary:*
- *dete* is the *-te* form of *deru* ("come out/emerge"); *yama (o) dete* is like "emerge(s) from (behind) the mountains, and . . ."
- *tera* = "temple" and *tera no ue* = "above/over the temple"
- . . . *ni kuru* = "comes to . . ." → *tera no ue ni kuru* = "comes over the temple."

霧にこゑ　　ごゑ学校の　　　形して
*Kiri ni koe*　　*–goe gakkō no*　　*katachi shite*

*Voices in the fog,*

*voices assuming a shape —*

*the shape of a school.*

Composed 1960.

Muikaichi-machi, in Shimane Prefecture, the town enveloped in dense fog. From the fog emerge children's voices, the voices of children in school. I hear the voices in the shape of a school.

---

◆　Season Word: *kiri*, "fog." Autumn, celestial phenomena.

*Vocabulary:*
- こゑ is the old spelling for こえ *koe* ("voice"); *koegoe* (the second *k* changes to *g* for euphony) makes it plural, and it also creates an irregular meter of 7-5-5.
- *katachi shite* is the *-te* form of *katachi (o) suru*, meaning to "form/take/be in (a certain) shape." Implied is the verb *kikoeru*, "hear": *gakkō no katachi shite (kikoeru)* = "(I hear) them in the shape of a school."

160

群山の　　中系なすは　　雪嶺のみ

*Gunzan no*　　*naka kei nasu wa*　　*yukine nomi*

## *A range of mountains*
## *in which the only ridges*
## *are of snowy peaks.*

Composed 1961.
In the Suzuka Mountains, the mountains are distributed in groups.
Among them is a snow-covered group of peaks, forming a line. In the
Suzuka Mountains, too, there is a Sierra Nevada (a snow-covered
mountain range).

---

✦　Season Word: *yuki*, "snow." Winter, celestial phenomena.

*Vocabulary:*
- *gunzan* combines the kanji for "group/crowd/flock/herd" and "mountain(s)."
  *gunzan no naka* = "among the several groups of mountains."
- 系 *kei* here is an abbreviation for 山系 *sankei*, "mountain range/group/system."
- *nasu* means "form/make" and *kei (o) nasu* means "form a range/group."
- *yukine* = "snow-covered peak" and *nomi* = "only," so *yukine nomi* = "only snow-covered peaks" — i.e., the group is made up entirely of snow-covered peaks.

161

美しき　　距離白鷺が　　蝶に見ゆ
*Utsukushiki*　　*kyori shirasagi ga*　　*chō ni miyu*

# *A pleasing distance*
## *that makes a white heron look*
## *like a butterfly.*

Composed 1961.
When I looked out from a rather high place on Mount Ibuki, I saw a
white butterfly fluttering off in the distance. When I looked carefully,
though, I realized it was a white heron. The distance that made a
heron look like a butterfly was a beautiful distance!

---

Season Word: *shirasagi*, "white heron." Summer, animals.

*Vocabulary:*
- *utsukushiki* is the classical *-ki* form of the adjective *utsukushii* ("beautiful"),
  modifying the noun, *kyori* ("distance").
- *miyu* is a classical equivalent of *mieru*, which in the expression . . . *ni mieru*
  means "appears/looks like . . ."

# ひぐらしが　鳴く奥能登の　ゆきどまり

*Higurashi ga　naku oku Noto no　yukidomari*

## *A clear cicada*
## *calling at the very end*
## *of outer Noto.*

Composed 1961.
When I went to Rokkō Point, on the Noto Peninsula, I heard a clear-toned cicada singing in a tree. It was at the very end of the Noto Peninsula. The cicada was singing out, protecting the place.

---

◆　Season Word: *higurashi*, "clear cicada." Autumn, animals.

*Vocabulary:*
- *higurashi ga naku* ("a clear cicada cries") can be thought of either as an independent sentence, or as a complete thought/sentence modifying *yukidomari*. In the latter case, *oku Noto no* ("in outer Noto") is a parallel modifier.
- *yukidomari* combines forms of *iku* ("go") and *tomaru* ("stop/halt") into a noun that essentially means "where the going stops" → "a dead end/the end of the road."

# 満月の　　紅き球体　出で来たる

Mangetsu no　akaki kyūtai　ide kitaru

## *Full moon arriving*
## *already taking the shape*
## *of a scarlet sphere.*

Composed 1961.
The full moon has arrived: its color is red; it is also a perfectly round celestial sphere. A full moon, barely into the sky as a scarlet sphere.

---

Season Word: *mangetsu*, "full moon." Autumn, celestial phenomena.

*Vocabulary:*
- *mangetsu* = "full moon"
- *akaki* is the classical *-ki* form of *akai* ("red").
- *kyūtai* combines the kanji for "ball" and "body," so it is literally like "spherical body" → "sphere."
- *ide kitaru* is equivalent to modern *dete kita*, the *-te* form of *deru* ("exit/emerge") and the past form of *kuru* ("come") → "came out/has come out."

明月の　　極小天に　　昇りつめ

*Meigetsu no　kyokushō ten ni　nobori tsume*

## *Full moon arriving*
## *at the spot in the heavens*
## *where it is smallest.*

Composed 1961.
The full moon was bright, pure white. It made its way through the
sky and reached its zenith. Since the moon was at its smallest there, I
realized that it was at its highest.

---

Season Word: *meigetsu*, "full moon." Autumn, celestial phenomena.

*Vocabulary:*
- *meigetsu* is literally "bright moon," but in poetry it usually refers to the full moon
  in the middle of the eighth month on the old lunar calendar, which generally
  comes sometime in September: "the harvest moon."
- *no* marks *meigetsu* as the subject, like *ga*.
- *kyokushō* = "minimum/smallest"
- *nobori* is from *noboru* ("climb"), and *tsume(ru)* after a verb implies that the ac-
  tion proceeds/is taken to its normal/logical culmination.
- 天 *ten* means "sky/heavens," so *ten ni noboru* = "climbs into the sky"; but it also
  suggests its homonym, 点 *ten*, meaning "point" → *kyokushō-ten* = "smallest
  point," and *kyokushō-ten ni noboru* = "climb to [its] smallest point."

鰭強く　　刎ねゐし鮪の　腸を抜く

*Hire tsuyoku*　　*hane-ishi shibi no*　　*wata o nuku*

## *Tuna being cleaned,*
## *and all the while the strong fins*
## *continue slapping.*

Composed 1961.
Tuna were being taken out of a boat, their fins still slapping. Fishermen in the market were ruthlessly disemboweling and gutting them. And the fish were still alive; their bowels were still alive!

---

Season Word: *shibi*, "tuna." Winter, animals.

*Vocabulary:*
- *hire* = "fins."
- *tsuyoku* is the adverb form of *tsuyoi* ("strong").
- *hane-ishi* is equivalent to modern *hanete-ita*, the past progressive form of *haneru* ("flip/flap"), so *hire tsuyoku hane-ishi* is literally "[they] were strongly flapping [their] fins." This complete thought/sentence modifies *shibi* ("tuna").
- 腸 *wata* (or more often *harawata*) means "intestines/bowels/entrails," and *nuku* is "pull/withdraw," so *wata o nuku* means "to gut and clean" the fish.

夜舟にて　魂魄通る　枯洲原
*Yobune nite　konpaku tōru　karesuhara*

*Island of brown reeds —*
*nightboat making its way past,*
*carrying a bier.*

Composed 1962.
When I saw the withered reeds on an island in the Yodo River, I had
a vivid vision of the scene of Bashō's remains being transported
upstream to Fushimi by nightboat.

---

Season Word: *karesu*, "island of brown reeds." Winter, topography.

*Vocabulary:*
- *nite* = "by/by means of."
- 魂 *kon* is "heart/spirit/soul" and 魄 *paku* is the form to which the spirit attaches, so *konpaku* essentially means "body and spirit." The context here shows it is a reference to Bashō's remains.

*Other points of interest:*
- Bashō died in Ōsaka in November 1694. The Yodo River originates in Lake Biwa and flows past Fushimi, Kyōto's outer port to Ōsaka Bay. Bashō's grave is at the Gichūji in Shiga Prefecture.

雪嶺に　発し海まで　短か川

*Setsurei ni　hasshi umi made　mijikagawa*

## *Off snowy mountains and down into the ocean, still a short river.*

Composed 1962.

I can see the snowy peak of Mount Tateyama. The melting snow forms rivers, which flow into the Japan Sea. It is only a short distance from the mountain to the sea. The river that began on the colossal mountain is a short river.

---

Season Word: *setsurei*, "snowy peak." Winter, topography.

*Vocabulary:*
- *hasshi* is the stem form of *hassuru*, meaning "depart/issue"; *setsurei ni hasshi* means "departs/issues from (the snowy peak), and . . ."
- *made* = "to/as far as."
- in the Japanese, *mijika* (from *mijikai*, "short") and *gawa* ("river"; *kawa* has changed to *gawa* for euphony) have been melded into a single word, something like "shortriver." Normal form here for an adjective modifying a noun would be *mijikaki kawa*.

168

山窪は　　蜜柑の花の　　匂ひ壺
*Yamakubo wa*　　*mikan no hana no*　　*nioitsubo*


# *A mountain hollow,*
# *becoming a sniffing bowl*
# *for mikan blossoms.*


Composed 1962.

I was walking along a road through mountains covered with mikan orchards and caught the scent of the blossoms coming from a mountain hollow. That hollow had trapped the scent. It was a sniffing bowl!

---

✦　Season Word: *mikan no hana*, "mikan blossom." Summer, plants.

*Vocabulary:*
- *yamakubo* = "mountain hollow."
- 匂ひ is the old spelling for 匂い *nioi* ("smell/scent/fragrance"), and *tsubo* = "vessel/bowl," so *nioitsubo* is "fragrance bowl" → "sniffing bowl."

*Other points of interest:*
- the *mikan* is the most important citrus fruit of Japan. It is sometimes called a "tangerine" or "mandarin orange" in English, but in fact is not quite the same as either of these. The Japanese eat great quantities of *mikan* — it is nearly impossible to eat just one. A popular travel snack, they are particularly noticeable on train platforms, packed six to a dozen in slim red-mesh bags.

170

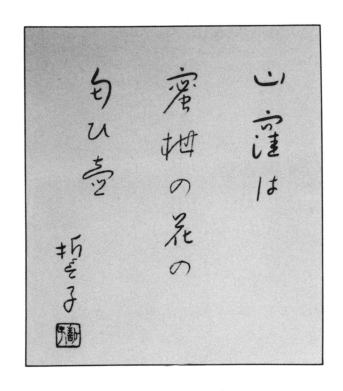

山窪は
蜜柑の花の
匂ひ壺

折々子

花蜜柑　　追風に香を　　焚きこめし
*Hanamikan*　　*oikaze ni ka o*　　*takikomeshi*

## *The mikan blossom —*
## *supplying the passing breeze*
## *with burning fragrance.*

Composed 1962.
The mikan blossoms exude a sweet scent. When the wind is blowing,
the fragrance rides on the wind and scents the wind. It is as if court
ladies of the Heian Era, who burned the fragrance of incense into
their robes, have scented the air as they passed.

---

◆　Season Word: *hanamikan*, "mikan blossom." Summer, plants.

*Vocabulary:*
- *oikaze* is literally "chasing wind" and can refer to any wind/breeze that is "carry-ing" something on it, including an aviator's "tailwind."
- *ka* = "scent/fragrance."
- *takikomeshi* is equivalent to modern *takikometa*, the past form of *takikomeru*. *Taki* is from *taku* ("burn") and adding *-komeru* to a verb indicates that the action is directed "into" something. As Seishi explains, the choice of this word comes from an association with the Heian courtiers' custom of "burning" fragrances into their robes by draping them over a frame and lighting incense under them. The Heian Era spanned from the end of the 8th to the end of the 12th century.

泳ぎより　歩行に移る　その境

*Oyogi yori　　hokō ni utsuru　　sono sakai*

# *That boundary line*
# *over which the swimmer moves*
# *when he starts to walk.*

Composed 1962.

I noticed that as a swimmer approaches the shore he changes his posture from horizontal to vertical, and starts to walk. The boundary line between swimming and standing is on the sandy ocean floor.

---

Season Word: *oyogi*, "swimming." Summer, life.

*Vocabulary:*
- *oyogi* is the noun form of *oyogu* ("swim").
- *yori* = "from" and *ni* = "to."
- *hokō* is a noun meaning "walking."
- *utsuru* = "shift/switch/change"; – *yori* – *ni utsuru* = "shift/change from – to –."
- *sakai* = "boundary," and *sono sakai* = "that boundary."

173

寒暁に　　鳴る指弾せし　かの鐘か
*Kangyō ni*　　*naru shidan seshi*　　*kano kane ka*

# *Bell in the cold dawn —*
# *is that the same bell I struck*
# *with my fingertips?*

Composed 1962.
At Senkō-ji Temple, in Onomichi, I flicked my fingertips against the great bell for announcing the hours. The next morning, in the cold dawn, I heard the sound of the bell from my bed. Was that the same bell that made the tiny sound when I struck it with my fingers?

---

✦　Season Word: *kangyō*, "cold dawn." Winter, season.

*Vocabulary:*
- *naru*, in reference to a bell, means "sound/ring/echo"; *kangyō ni naru* = "sounds/ rings in the cold dawn."
- 指弾 *shidan* is a combination of kanji meaning "finger" and "strike/hit/play [an instrument]." *Shidan seshi* is a classical equivalent of *shidan shita*, past form of *shidan suru* ("strike/flick with fingers"). Adding a form of *suru* to a noun describing an action makes it a verb.
- *kano* is a classical equivalent of *ano* ("that"): *kano kane ka* = "is it that bell?"

雪降るな　人間魚雷　いまぼろぼろ

*Yuki furu na*　*ningen gyorai*　*ima boroboro*

## *Let there be no snow —*
## *for the human torpedo*
## *is now in tatters.*

Composed 1962.

I looked at the human torpedo at Etajima — a badly deteriorated
human torpedo. Oh, for the souls of the young men who piloted
them! It threatened to snow then, so I called out to the sky: "Let there
be no snow on this tattered human torpedo!"

---

Season Word: *yuki*, "snow." Winter, celestial phenomena.

*Vocabulary:*
- *furu* = "[rain/snow] falls," and *na* is a particle for prohibition ("don't –"), so *yuki furu na* = "don't snow."
- *boroboro* = "tattered/in tatters."

*Other points of interest:*
- the manned torpedo, which Seishi saw at the former Naval Academy at Etajima, was one of the suicide weapons used to defend the Japanese mainland in World War II. It had some success in disrupting Allied supply routes.

175

天耕の　峯に達して　峯を越す
Tenkō no　　mine ni tasshite　　mine o kosu

# *Having farmed the land*
# *to its summit, now they start*
# *down the other side.*

Composed 1962.
I saw Kurahashi Island beyond the straits. They say in Chinese,
"Farming the land to the heavens." On the island they seem to have
cultivated to the top of the mountain, and then continued over on the
other side. The intensity of the cultivation.

---

✦　Season Word: *kō*, "cultivating." Spring, life.

*Vocabulary:*
- *ten* = "sky/heavens" and *kō* = "cultivation/cultivating," making *tenkō* a noun that means "cultivation to the heavens." *No* marks this as the subject, like *ga*.
- *tasshite* is the *-te* form of *tassuru* ("arrives at/reaches/attains"); *mine ni tasshite* = "reaches the summit, and . . ."
- *kosu* = "surpasses/surmounts/goes over."

瞬間に　　彎曲の鉄　　寒曝し
*Shunkan ni　　wankyoku no tetsu　kanzarashi*

*The iron framework*
*twisted in a moment's time*
*bleaches in the cold.*

Composed 1962.
When I visited the Atom Bomb Dome, in Hiroshima, what impressed
me most was the iron frame of the dome, twisted in the twinkling of
an eye by the atomic bomb. It stood there assaulted by the cold air.

Season Word: *kanzarashi*, "exposed to the cold." Winter, life.

*Vocabulary:*
- *shunkan* = "an instant," and *shunkan ni* = "in an instant."
- *wankyoku* = "a curve/a bend," so *wankyoku no tetsu* is "bent iron/steel" →
  "twisted iron."
- *kanzarashi* combines the kanji for "cold" and "expose" for a noun meaning
  "exposure to the cold" → "be exposed to/weather/bleach in the cold."

*Other points of interest:*
- the Atom Bomb Dome is the remains of the Industry Promotion Hall in Hiro-
  shima, which stands within the Atom Bomb Memorial Park and is the only ruin
  that has been preserved at the hypocenter of the bomb blast.

蜜柑山　　南へ袖を　　両開き

*Mikan'yama*　　*minami e sode o*　　*ryōbiraki*

# A *mikan mountain*
### *throwing her two sleeves out wide*
### *as she faces south.*

Composed 1962.

I looked at the mikan mountain in Shimotsu-kitsumoto. The mountain
was split vertically by a crease, with a mikan mountain on either side.
It was as if the mountain had spread its kimono sleeves to receive the
rays of the southern sun.

---

✦ Season Word: *mikan,* "mikan." Winter, plants.

*Vocabulary:*
- strictly speaking, *mikan* is different from both the tangerine and the mandarin or-
  ange, but these are still the most common names used in English for this Japanese
  citrus fruit. *Mikan* groves are most commonly found on hills/mountainsides.
- *e* = "to/toward."
- *sode* = "sleeves."
- *ryō* = "both" and *-biraki* (changed from *hiraki* for euphony) is from *hiraku*
  ("open/spread out"), so *sode o ryōbiraki* means "spreads both sleeves." We are to
  imagine broad kimono sleeves spread wide.

寒庭に　　在る石更に　　省くべし
*Kantei ni*　　*aru ishi sara ni*　　*habuku beshi*

# *In the cold garden,*
## *they really should have left out*
### *more of the stones!*

Composed 1962.

The stone garden of the Ryōan-ji, in Kyōto. In the cold garden, 15 stones are arranged in groups of 7, 5, and 3. Fifteen is the smallest number possible, but it seems to me, accustomed to working in the short poetic form of the haiku, that more stones should have been left out.

---

Season Word: *kantei*, "cold garden." Winter, topography.

*Vocabulary:*
- *kantei ni aru* is a complete thought/sentence ("are in the cold garden") modifying *ishi* ("stones").
- *sara ni* = "more/again."
- *habuku* = "exclude/omit/eliminate," and *beshi* is a classical form implying "ought to/should," so *habuku beshi* literally means "ought to exclude/eliminate." The intended meaning, though, is that more stones "could have been left out, " rather than that they should now be eliminated.

*Other points of interest:*
- the Ryōan-ji garden is the best known of Japan's gardens in the Zen style.

179

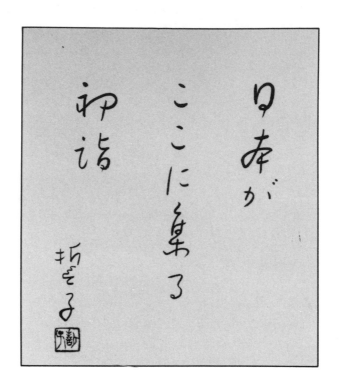

日本が　　ここに集まる　　初詣
*Nippon ga*　　*koko ni atsumaru*　　*hatsumōde*

*Here all of Japan*
*comes together to perform*
*its first pilgrimage.*

Composed 1963.
The first pilgrimage of the year to the Inner Shrine at Ise. As I walk toward the Main Hall, I pass returning pilgrims. They are people who have come from all over, every corner of Japan. All Japan gathers here.

---

✦　Season Word: *hatsumōde*, "first pilgrimage of the year." New Year's, observances.

*Vocabulary:*
- *Nippon ga koko ni atsumaru* ("Japan gathers here") can be thought of either as a complete sentence ending in a colon, or as a complete sentence directly modifying *hatsumōde*.

*Other points of interest:*
- the Ise Shrine is generally regarded as the most important Shintō shrine. The shrine comprises an Inner Shrine and Outer Shrine as well as several other affiliated shrines. Visits there are particularly heavy in auspicious years.

真珠作業　場絶対に　静止の海
Shinju sagyō　　–jō zettai-ni　　seishi no umi

*A center for pearl*
*processing, absolutely*
*a pacific sea.*

Composed 1963.
The pearl farm is in a little cove, where the boat in which the pearls
are shelled rides at anchor. The sea is entirely calm, a complete calm
for the sake of the pearl shells.

---

◆　Season Word: *shinju sagyō*, "pearl industry processing." Summer, life.

*Vocabulary:*
- *shinju* = "pearl."
- *sagyō* = "work/operations/processing," and *sagyōjō* = "place of work/opera-
  tions/processing."
- *zettai-ni* = "absolutely/positively."
- *seishi*, combining kanji for "quiet" and "is stopped/still," means "stillness/re-
  pose."

炎天に　　清流熱き　　湯なれども
*Enten ni*　　*seiryū atsuki*　　*yu naredomo*

# *In the summer heat,*
## *looking like a cool current —*
### *this hot spring water.*

Composed 1963.
It was the hot season. Hot water gushed from the fountainhead at the
Yuzaki Hot Springs. At first glance, the water seemed fresh and cool.
The gushing hot spring water seemed strangely like clear, cool water.

---

◆　Season Word: *enten,* "summer heat." Summer, celestial phenomena.

*Vocabulary:*
- *enten* combines kanji for "flames" and "sky/heavens/weather"; *enten ni* = "under
  a flaming sky/in flaming weather."
- *seiryū* is literally "clear flow/stream," but also implies a cool stream.
- *atsuki* is the classical *-ki* form of *atsui* ("hot"), modifying *yu* ("hot water").
- *naredomo* is a classical form meaning "even though it is," so *atsuki yu naredomo*
  means "even though it is hot water." The syntax is inverted. Normal order would
  be *atsuki yu naredomo, enten ni seiryū,* "Even though it is hot water, (it looks
  like) a cool stream on/for a hot day."

*Other points of interest:*
- the Japanese enjoy hot spring resorts at all times of the year.

183

懸崖菊　　いかな高さに　置くならん
Kengaigiku　　ikana takasa ni　　oku naran

## *The better to show*
## *a chrysanthemum cascade,*
## *how high must it be?*

Composed 1963.
In a chrysanthemum garden, a chrysanthemum show was taking
place. A chrysanthemum cascade was in a stand on the ground. When
I looked at it, I wondered about the proper height to show chrysan-
themums. How high should it be?

---

Season Word: *kiku*, "chrysanthemum." Autumn, plants.

*Vocabulary:*
- *kengai* is "cliff/precipice," and *giku* (changed from *kiku* for euphony) means
  "chrysanthemum" → "chrysanthemum cascade."
- *ikana* is short for *ikanaru*, an archaic equivalent of *donna* ("what kind of"), and
  *takasa* is the noun form of *takai* ("high"): *ikana takasa* = "what kind of height?"
  → "what height?"
- *oku* = "to set/place," and *naran* used in a question is like modern . . . *no darō ka*,
  "I wonder what/who/etc.": *ikana takasa ni oku naran* = "I wonder at what height
  [they] will place it?"

184

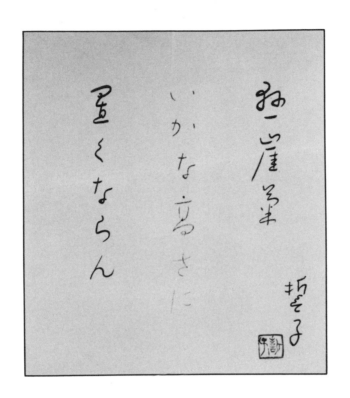

隅の隅　　にてラグビーの　最後の勝

*Sumi no sumi*　　*nite ragubii no*　　*saigo no kachi*

## *Deep in a corner*
## *of a corner, a rugby*
## *game is decided.*

Composed 1964.

The rugby game went on and on. In a corner of the field, friend and foe battled. There the final victor was decided. The rugby game was won in a corner.

---

Season Word: *ragubii,* "rugby." Winter, life.

*Vocabulary:*
- *sumi* = "corner/nook," and *sumi no sumi* is like "the farthest corner of a corner."
- *nite* indicates the place where something occurs: "at/in."
- *saigo* = "last/final."
- *kachi* = "victory," and *saigo no kachi* = "the final victory."

拭くことも　なし全車窓　息曇る
*Fuku koto mo*　*nashi zen shasō*　*ikigumoru*

## *Train windows clouded*
## *with passengers' breath, and yet*
## *no one wipes them off.*

Composed 1964.
A passenger coach in motion. Since it was cold outside, all the windows were covered with the breath of the passengers. Yet nobody wiped it off. Because of that breath, the scenery outside was invisible.

---

Season Word: *ikigumoru*, "become clouded with breath." Winter, life.

*Vocabulary:*
- *fuku* = "wipe."
- *nashi* is the classical form of negative *nai*, and . . . *koto ga/mo nai* is an expression meaning ". . . doesn't occur/never happens/isn't done." *Fuku koto mo nashi* = "no one wipes [them]."
- *zen* = "all/every," and *shasō* combines the kanji for "car" and "window," so *zen shasō* means "all the [train] car windows."

武具飾る　光る眼も手も　足もなし
Bugu kazaru　hikaru me mo te mo　ashi mo nashi

*Armor on display —*
*nowhere an arm or a leg,*
*or a shining eye.*

Composed 1964.
The Boy's Festival, in May. A suit of armor has been placed on a chest, with a helmet above it. It looks like a samurai sitting on the chest, but no eye gleams out of the helmet; neither hand nor foot protrudes from the armor.

.

Season Word: *bugu kazaru*, "to display armor." Summer, observances.

*Vocabulary:*
- *bugu* is literally "military equipment/tools" and can refer to both "weapons" and "armor" — here the latter.
- *kazaru* = "display."
- *hikaru* ("to shine/glow") modifies *me* ("eye"): *hikaru me* = "shining eye."
- *nashi* is the classical form of *nai* ("not have/not exist"), and the series – *mo* – *mo* – *mo nashi* is like "[it] has neither – nor – nor –."

*Other points of interest:*
- displays of armor and other masculine gear are common on Children's Day, formerly Boys' Day, celebrated on May 5.

白毫は　　白万緑を　　凝らすとも

*Byakugō wa　shiro banryoku o　korasu to mo*

## Buddha's jewel is white,
## even though the green leaves' shades
## concentrate in it.

Composed 1964.
At a temple in the green leaves season, the image of the Buddha
reflects the foliage. Yet the jewel in the Buddha's forehead remains
white. No matter how much the green leaves concentrate in it, the
jewel goes on being white.

---

✦　Season Word: *banryoku*, "green leaves." Summer, plants.

*Vocabulary:*
- *byakugō* refers to a white curl between the Buddha's eyebrows, which on images
  of the Buddha is often represented by a crystal jewel: *byakugō wa shiro* = "the
  Buddha's white curl/jewel is white."
- *banryoku* is literally "all things are green" (see page 157), but here it is being
  used more like "the green of all things."
- *korasu* = "concentrate/focus [something]," so *banryoku o korasu* = "concentrate/
  focus the green of all things."
- *to mo* = "even if," so *korasu to mo* is essentially similar to modern *korashite mo*,
  "even if [it] is concentrated/focused." The syntax is inverted.

山車統べて　　鎧皇后　　立ち給ふ
*Dashi subete*　　*yoroikōgō*　　*tachitamō*

## *Ruling over all*
## *festival carts, the Empress*
## *stands in her armor.*

Composed 1964.
The Ishitori Festival, in Kuwana. The Empress Jingō, clad in armor, stands on a festival cart. Many carts follow hers, but the Empress in armor rules over all.

---

✦　Season Word: *dashi*, "festival float." Summer, observances.

*Vocabulary:*
- *subete* is from *suberu*, meaning "be in charge/control" → "rule." *Dashi* ("festival floats") is the object of this verb: "controlling/ruling the festival floats . . ."
- *yoroi* = "armor," and *kōgō* = "empress"; *yoroi kōgō* = "empress in armor." The particle *ga*, to mark the subject, has been omitted after this phrase.
- *tachi* is from *tatsu*, "stand," and *-tamō* is an honorific suffix. 給ふ(=たまふ) is the old spelling of 給う(=たもう), but even with the old spelling the word was pronounced *tamō*.

舟虫の　　猪ひ深き　日本海
*Funamushi no　utagaibukaki　Nihonkai*

## *On the Japan Sea,*
### *where all the sea lice reside*
### *deep in suspicion.*

Composed 1964.
When I went to the Japan Sea, I found the beaches swarming with sea lice. They watched me — ever ready to flee. The Japan Sea lice are very suspicious.

---

Season Word: *funamushi*, "sea lice." Summer, animals.

*Vocabulary:*
- *no* marks the subject, like *ga*; even in modern Japanese this is a common substitution within modifying clauses.
- *utagaibukaki* is from *utagau* ("doubt/be suspicious of") and *fukai* ("deep"; *f* changes to *b* for euphony, and it is in the classical *-ki* form for modifying a noun) → "deeply suspicious."
- the first two lines are equivalent to the modern Japanese *funamushi ga utagaibukai* ("the sea lice are deeply suspicious"), a complete thought/sentence modifying *Nihon-kai* ("The Japan Sea").

瀬に沁みて　奈良までとどく　蝉のこゑ

*Se ni shimite*　　*Nara made todoku*　　*semi no koe*

## *Cicadas' voices*
## *soaking in the cool current*
## *as far as Nara.*

Composed 1964.

It is said that the water for Nara's water-drawing ceremony comes from the Unose stream, in Onyū. The voices of the cicadas singing now are soaking into Unose waters and making their way to Nara with the underground current.

---

◆　Season Word: *semi*, "cicada." Summer, animals.

*Vocabulary:*
- *se* = "(river) current"
- *shimite* is the *-te* form of *shimiru* ("penetrate/soak into/become infused in").
- *todoku* = "reach/be delivered to"
- *se ni shimite Nara made todoku* ("[It] soaks into the current and reaches/goes all the way to Nara") can be thought of as modifying *semi no koe* ("cicada's voices") or as set off with a colon.
- こゑ is the old spelling of こえ. The difference in pronunciation between え *e* and ゑ *we* disappeared quite early, but the distinction continued to be made in writing, and ゑ remained in the *wa* column of the kana charts until after World War II. Many Japanese schooled before the war continue to use ゑ today.

192

刈田行く　　電車の裡も　　刈田なり

*Karita yuku　　densha no uchi mo　　karita nari*

*Harvested rice fields*
*within and without this train*
*traveling through them.*

Composed 1964.
I was passing through harvested fields in a train. To the right and the
left, the fields were cut clean. The harvest fields even came into the
train. The inside of the train became a cut-over field. Perhaps the
train invited the fields in.

---

Season Word: *karita*, "harvested rice fields." Autumn, topography.

*Vocabulary:*
- *karita* is from *karu* ("cut/reap/harvest") and *ta* ("rice paddy/field") → "harvested rice fields."
- *yuku* is an alternate form of *iku* ("go"). The particle *o*, which would here mean "along/through," has been omitted before *yuku*.
- *uchi* = "inside," and *mo* = "also," so *uchi mo* = "the inside also" → "even the inside/even in."
- *nari* is a classical equivalent of *da/desu* ("is").

蓮瓣の　　崩れてゐるは　　この世なり

*Renben no*　　*kuzurete-iru wa*　　*kono yo nari*

# *This world is the place*
# *of the disintegration*
# *of lotus petals.*

Composed 1964.
The petals of the lotuses in the pond have fallen. The blossoms in the
Buddha's picture stand all about the central stem. One cannot believe
that the lotus petals that have fallen belong to the other world.

---

Season Word: *ren*, "lotus." Summer, plants.

*Vocabulary:*
- *ren* = "lotus," and *ben* = "petal."
- 崩れてゐる is the old spelling of 崩れている *kuzurete-iru* ("have/are fallen"), from *kuzureru* ("crumble/fall/lose[their] shape"). ゐ formerly belonged to the *wa* column of the kana chart (see page 192).
- *wa* makes the complete sentence *renben no kuzurete-iru* ("the lotus petals are fallen") function as a noun, and as the topic of the longer sentence: "as for the fallen lotus petals, . . ."
- *nari* is a classical equivalent of *da/desu* ("is/are"), so *kono yo nari* is literally "[they] are this world." As Seishi indicates, he also intended the meaning "[they] are <u>of</u> this world."

194

殺生石　　雪もこの世の　　ものならず

*Sesshōseki*　　*yuki mo kono yo no*　　*mono narazu*

# At the Murder Rock,
# even the snow on the ground
# is not of this world.

Composed 1965.
The Murder Rock, in Nasu, gives off poisonous hydrogen sulfide gas.
All kinds of insects are killed by it. It is hell for insects. I looked at
the snow there, and it seemed to be the snow of hell.

---

Season Word: *yuki*, "snow." Winter, celestial phenomena.

*Vocabulary:*
- *sesshō* is literally "killing of life," and *seki* = "stone/rock" → "murder rock."
- *kono yo* = "this world," and *kono yo no mono* = "a thing of this world."
- *narazu* is the negative form of *nari*, equivalent to modern Japanese *da/desu* ("is")
  → "is not." *kono yo no mono narazu* = "is not a thing of this world."

*Other points of interest:*
- an elaborate legend of conspiracy, murder, and placation of a vengeful spirit sur-
  rounds a lava flow, near Nasu Hot Springs in Tochigi Prefecture, which contin-
  ues to emit poisonous and other gasses from its pores. One particular rock there
  came to be known as "Murder Rock."

高館に　雪その雪を　握り潰す

*Takadachi ni　yuki sono yuki o　nigiri tsubusu*

## *Takadachi snow —*
## *I picked up some of that snow,*
## *squeezed and crumbled it.*

Composed 1965.

The site in Hiraizumi where Yoshitsune stayed. Yoshitsune came expecting the assistance of the Fujiwaras, but Fujiwara Yasuhira attacked and brought about Yoshitsune's death. I took some of the snow there in my hand and squeezed it to vent my anger.

---

Season Word: *yuki*, "snow." Winter, celestial phenomena.

*Vocabulary:*
- *Takadachi* is one of the names given to the residence built for Minamoto Yoshitsune by Fujiwara Hidehira (Yasuhira's father) near Hiraizumi (see below).
- *nigiri* is from *nigiru* ("grip/hold/squeeze [in one's hand/fist]").
- *tsubusu* = "mash/crush/crumble."

*Other points of interest:*
- Yoshitsune is one of the greatest heroes of Japanese history and legend. As a result of a dispute with his half-brother, Minamoto Yoritomo, Japan's first shogun ruler, he sought and found refuge with Fujiwara Hidehira in northern Japan, but was attacked in 1189 by the son Yasuhira after Hidehira's death.

卒塔婆もて　　雪除となす　　奥の院
*Sotoba mote*　　*yukiyoke to nasu*　　*oku no in*

## *Holy of holies —*
## *where the stupas of the dead*
## *become snow fences.*

Composed 1965.
I climbed to the holiest temple of Yamadera, following the path of
Bashō. Stupas of the dead were set up in rows there and became snow
fences. Stupas of the dead as snow fences.

---

Season Word: *yukiyoke*, "snow fence." Winter, life.

*Vocabulary:*
- *sotoba* = "stupa."
- *mote* = "with/using/by means of."
- *yukiyoke* = "snow fence," and *nasu* = "to make/form."
- *sotoba mote yukiyoke to nasu* = "make a snow fence with stupas."
- *oku* = "the inner/innermost part."
- *in* is one of several words used for Buddhist "temples/halls/buildings." *Oku no in* is literally "the innermost temple/hall."

海の上　　飛ぶ雪嶺の　　加護もなく
*Umi no ue*　　*tobu setsurei no*　　*kago mo naku*

***Flight over water —***
***the gods of snowy mountains***
***have no power here.***

Composed 1965.
I was flying over snowy peaks and thinking we were flying under the protection of those peaks. Then we left them and flew over the ocean. The snowy peaks have no authority there.

---

Season Word: *setsurei*, "snowy peak." Winter, topography.

*Vocabulary:*
- *umi no ue* = "over the sea/ocean"
- *tobu* = "fly"
- *kago* means "divine protection." *Setsurei no kago* ("divine protection of the snowy mountains/peaks") reflects the Shintō belief that there is divinity in all of nature; mountains have an especially prominent place in this belief.

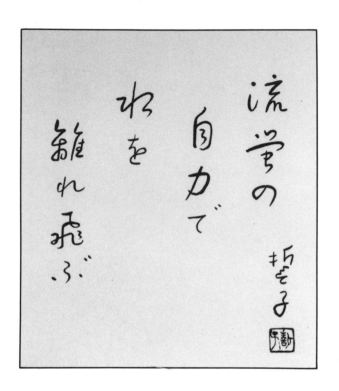

流蛍の
自力で
水を
離れ飛ぶ

哲子

流螢の　　自力で水を　　離れ飛ぶ

*Ryūkei no*　　*jiriki de mizu o*　　*hanare tobu*

## *Floating firefly*
## *moving out of the water*
## *by its own power.*

Composed 1965.

A lighted firefly floats on the river. Ordinarily, he would keep on floating with the current, but now he gathers himself together and takes off. He leaves the water under his own power.

---

◆　Season Word: *kei*, "firefly." Summer, animals.

*Vocabulary:*
- *ryūkei* is literally "flowing firefly" → "floating firefly."
- *jiriki* = "one's own power," and *jiriki de* = "by/under one's own power."
- *o* marks the point of departure.
- *hanare* is from *hanareru* ("separate/part/depart from"), and *tobu* = "fly": *hanare tobu* = "fly away from."

猪吊るす　生きてゐし牙　きたなけれ
*Shishi tsurusu*　　*ikite-ishi kiba*　　*kitanakere*

## *On a hook he hangs —*
## *the wild boar, much as he lived,*
## *with his dirty tusks.*

Composed 1966.
A wild boar has been shot and hangs under the eaves. I noticed his dirty tusks. They were that dirty, the tusks he used to root up grubby fare.

---

Season Word: *shishi*, "wild boar." Summer, animals.

*Vocabulary:*
- *shishi*, or more commonly, *inoshishi*, is "wild boar." *Shishi (o) tsurusu* is literally "hang up a wild boar," but here the meaning is essentially "a wild boar hangs/is hanging."
- 生きてゐし *ikite-ishi* is equivalent to modern Japanese *ikite-ita*, the past form of *ikite-iru* ("is living"). Here the phrase implies "like when it was living."
- *kitanakere* is a classical form of *kitanai* ("dirty/filthy") that has an emphatic feeling.

202

悴む手　女は千も　万も擦る

*Kajikamu te　onna wa sen mo　man mo suru*

## *She rubs her cold hands a thousand times, even ten thousand times over.*

Composed 1966.

A woman rubs her hands together to rid them of cold. She does it a thousand, even ten thousand times. She doesn't care if people see her. She does it as if it is a feminine prerogative.

---

Season Word: *kajikamu*, "be numb with cold." Winter, life.

*Vocabulary:*
- *suru* = "rub"; the object of this verb is *kajikamu te* ("hands that are numb with cold").
- *mo* is used after numbers/quantities to emphasize that that number/quantity is large, so *sen mo man mo* is like "a whole thousand times, even a whole ten-thousand times."

月読の　　国へ月山　　より登る
*Tsukiyomi no　kuni e Gassan　　yori noboru*

# *From Gassan Mountain,*
# *I ascend to the heaven*
# *of Tsukiyomi.*

Composed 1966.
I climbed Mount Gassan, one of the Three Mountains of Dewa. The
shrine on top is dedicated to the deity Tsukuyomi. Praying with
folded hands, I felt as if I could climb from there into the world of the
moon. My heart leapt to heaven.

---

Season Word: *noboru,* "to climb (mountains)." Summer, life.

*Vocabulary:*
- the names *Tsukiyomi* and *Gassan* both contain 月, the kanji for "moon," and the
  poem is built on the association this establishes.
- *e* = "to," so *Tsukiyomi no kuni e* = "to the land of [the deity] Tsukiyomi" → "to
  Tsukiyomi's heaven." Also implied is *tsuki no kuni e,* "to the land of the moon."
- *yori* = "from," so *Gassan yori* is "from Gassan."

*Other points of interest:*
- the shrines at the summits of the Three Mountains of Dewa Province are particu-
  larly sacred to members of the Shugendō sect, whose faith centers around moun-
  tains.

204

滝川の　　中行く登山　道なれば
*Takikawa no　naka yuku tozan　-michi nareba*

### *Since this mountain road*
### *goes up a rushing river,*
### *I climb a river.*

Composed 1966.
A rapid stream cuts across the road from Mount Gassan to Mount Yudonosan, so I walked through it. Since it is the road up the mountain, climbers must take it even if it becomes a rushing river.

---

Season Word: *tozanmichi*, "road up a mountain." Summer, life.

*Vocabulary:*
- *taki* can refer either to a "waterfall" or to steep "rapids," and *kawa* is "river/stream," so *takikawa* gives the image of a rocky/rushing stream tumbling down a mountainside. *Takikawa no naka (o) yuku* = "go/goes through a rushing stream."
- *nareba* is a *-ba* form of classical *nari*, which is equivalent to modern *da/desu* ("is"). This *-ba* form can mean either "because/since" or "when," depending on the context — in this case the former: "because/since it is [a road that goes through a rushing river]."
- in Japanese, the end of the poem links back to the beginning for a literal meaning something like: "Because the road up the mountain goes through a rushing river, I go/walk/climb through a rushing river."

海水着　　脱げば出生　　以来の白
*Kaisuigi*　　*nugeba shusshō*　　*irai no shiro*

***Under my swimsuit,***
***a whiteness that has not changed***
***since my natal day.***

Composed 1966.
I went swimming and got sunburned. When I took my suit off, and the
white skin hidden by the suit appeared, the line between the tanned
skin and the white skin was clearly discernible. It was a whiteness that
had not changed since I was born.

---

Season Word: *kaisuigi*, "swimsuit." Summer, life.

*Vocabulary:*
- *nugeba* is a classical *-ba* form of *nugu* ("take off/remove [an article of cloth-ing]"). This *-ba* form can mean either "because" or "when" — in this case the latter.
- *shusshō* = "birth," and *shusshō irai* = "since birth."

白鷺の　　顎ひきしめて　飛ぶは嘉し

*Shirasagi no　　ago hikishimete　　tobu wa yoshi*

## *What a sight to see:*
## *heron pulling in his chin*
## *as he flies away.*

Composed 1966.
When I climbed Mount Hirasan, I saw a heron flying in front of me. He
had his chin tucked in and flew with great determination. I looked at
his expression and said, "Great."

---

Season Word: *shirasagi,* "white heron." Summer, animals.

*Vocabulary:*
- *ago* = "chin"
- *hikishimete* is the *-te* form of *hikishimeru* ("pull in/draw together/tighten").
- *wa* marks the full preceding clause as the topic of the sentence: "As for the white heron flying with his chin tucked in, . . ."
- *yoshi,* the classical form of *ii/yoi* ("good/fine/great"), continues to be used idiomatically in modern Japanese, especially as an interjection/exclamation.

# 山上湖　掌にて平して　船遊び

*Sanjōko　　te nite narashite　　funaasobi*

## *A ride in a boat,*
## *smoothing down the mountain lake*
## *with palm of one hand.*

Composed 1966.
A man-made mountain lake. I rode in a pleasure boat around the lake trailing my hand and smoothing the lake water. Caressing the lake with the palm of my hand, I became one with it.

---

◆　Season Word: *funaasobi*, "boatride." Summer, life.

*Vocabulary:*
- *sanjō* = "mountaintop," so *sanjōko* would literally be "mountaintop lake" → "mountain lake."
- *te* means "hand/arm," but 掌, usually read *tanagokoro* or *tenohira*, means "palm."
- *nite* = "with/by means of"
- *narashite* is the *-te* form of *narasu* ("to smooth/level/make even").
- *funaasobi* is from *fune* ("boat") and the noun form of *asobu* ("play/enjoy oneself").

# 強きもの　扁平の頭の　大山椒魚

*Tsuyoki mono*　*henpei no zu no*　*ōhanzaki*

## *Powerful creature —*
## *a giant salamander*
## *with a broad flat head.*

Composed 1966.
The giant salamander is called either *sanshōuo* or *hanzaki* in Japanese.
It has a broad flat head and can spring with terrific force. The giant
salamander, with his broad flat head, is a powerful creature.

---

✦　Season Word: *hanzaki*, "salamander." Summer, animals.

*Vocabulary:*
- *tsuyoki* is the classical *-ki* form of *tsuyoi* ("strong/powerful"), modifying *mono* ("thing," or, in this case, "creature").
- *henpei* = "flatness," and *zu* = "head," so *henpei no zu* is literally "head of flatness" → " flat head."
- *ō-* is the prefix form of *ōkii* ("big/large") → *ōhanzaki* = "giant salamander"; *henpei no zu no ōhanzaki* = "giant salamander with a broad flat head."

登山口　　鳥居の額の　　俯向くも
*Tozanguchi*　　*torii no gaku no*　　*utsumuku mo*

## *The start of a climb —*
## *tablet of a torii*
## *tilting toward me.*

Composed 1966.
On a trip to the Omogo Valley, I stood at the starting point for the climb up Mount Ishizuchi. There was a torii there, with a tablet tilting my way. It spoke to me: "Pass under and start climbing."

---

Season Word: *tozan*, "mountain climbing." Summer, life.

*Vocabulary:*
- 口 -*guchi* (from *kuchi*, "mouth/opening") used as a suffix means "entrance/opening to/starting point for."
- *utsumuku* = "face downwards"
- *mo* is an emphatic particle that often adds emotional overtones, in this case perhaps a combination of gratification and excitement: "[it] even faces down toward me!/[it] even tilts my way!"

登山道　　一歩より急　　天まで急
*Tozanmichi*　　*ippo yori kyū*　　*ten made kyū*

# *Road up the mountain —*
## *steep grade from the starting point*
## *steep grade to heaven.*

Composed 1966.
I went through the torii, my first step up the trail. It was steep from that first step. I looked up and saw that it was the same grade all the way to the sky.

---

Season Word: *tozanmichi*, "road up a mountain." Summer, life.

*Vocabulary:*
- *ippo* = "one step," or, in this case, "first step."
- *yori* = "from," and *made* = "to/as far as"
- *kyū*, when referring to the grade of hill/slope, means "steep." *Ippo yori kyū* = "steep from the first step," and *ten made kyū* = "steep to the sky/heavens."

水盤の　　ぐるりに月を　　滴らす
*Suiban no*　　*gururi ni tsuki o*　　*shitatarasu*

***Everywhere about***
***the copper lotus basin***
***moonlight is dripping.***

Composed 1966.
One moonlit night, I climbed a mountain to an old temple. Beside the temple staircase was a copper basin in the shape of a lotus, with water dripping from its brim. The moon lit up the water, making the basin drip moonlight.

Season Word: *tsuki*, "moon." Autumn, celestial phenomena.

*Vocabulary:*
- *suiban* = "water basin."
- *gururi* = "surroundings/the area all around," so *suiban no gururi* means "all around/everywhere about the water basin."
- *shitatarasu* means "make/cause/allow to drip," and *suiban no* can be read as the subject of this verb, so *suiban no tsuki o shitatarasu* becomes "the water basin makes/lets the moonlight drip."

月よりも　上空を飛ぶ　白鳥座

*Tsuki yori mo*　　*jōkū o tobu*　　*Hakuchōza*

## *Higher than the moon,*
## *the white swan constellation*
## *flying through the sky.*

Composed 1966.
The northern cross was visible in a moonlit sky. The cross described
a white swan with wings spread. Since the moon was bright and
appeared close, that constellation was like a white swan flying higher
than the moon.

---

Season Word: *tsuki*, "moon." Autumn, celestial phenomena.

*Vocabulary:*
- *yori mo* = "even more than," here implying "even higher than."
- *jōkū* = "upper sky/the sky overhead," and . . . *yori mo jōkū* = "even higher in the sky than . . ."
- *jōkū o tobu* = "fly overhead."
- *hakuchō* is literally "white bird" → "swan"; *-za* is a suffix meaning "constellation."
- *tsuki yori mo jōkū o tobu* is a complete thought/sentence ("flies higher than the moon") that can be thought of either as modifying *Hakuchōza* or as set off with a colon.

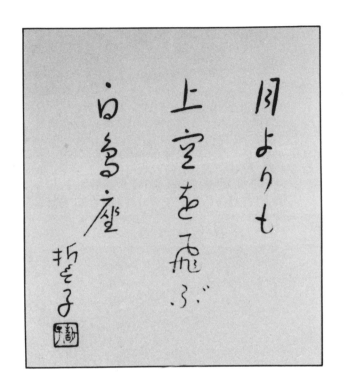

月よりも
上空を飛ぶ
白鳥座
哲もう子

215

西までの　　天路月にも　　遙かなる

*Nishi made no　　tenro tsuki ni mo　　haruka naru*

## *Even for the moon*
## *the heavenly journey west*
## *is a distant one.*

Composed 1966.
The moon came out of the mountains. It still had to go all the way to
the west. The path through the heavens is a long, long one, even for
the moon.

---

Season Word: *tsuki*, "moon." Autumn, celestial phenomena.

*Vocabulary:*
- *nishi* = "west," and *nishi made* "to/as far as the west" → "to the western horizon."
- *tenro* = "heavenly path/journey."
- *ni mo* = "even for": *tsuki ni mo* = "even for the moon."
- *haruka naru* is equivalent to modern *haruka da/desu* ("is distant/far").

# 廃山家　露霜解けて　滴れり
## Haisanga　tsuyujimo tokete　shitatareri

*Decayed mountain house —*
*frozen dewdrops melting out,*
*then dripping to earth.*

Composed 1966.
A dilapidated, deserted house in the mountains. The eaves were still intact, and the melting frost dripped from them. That faint movement in a rotting house in the mountains.

---

Season Word: *tsuyujimo*, "frozen dew." Autumn, celestial phenomena.

*Vocabulary:*
- 廃 *hai* means "obsolete/decayed/abandoned," and 山家 *sanga* is a combination of "mountain" and "house."
- 露 *tsuyu* = "dew," and 霜 *shimo* = "frost"; *tsuyujimo* (*sh* changes to *j* for euphony) = "frozen dew."
- *tokete* is the *-te* form of *tokeru* ("melt/dissolve").
- *shitatareri* is a classical equivalent of *shitatatte-iru*, the progressive form of *shitataru* ("to drip") → "is dripping."

217

街道に　　障子を閉めて　紙一重
*Kaidō ni*　　*shōji o shimete*　*kami hitoe*

## Along the high road,
### sliding doors closed to the world,
### but one page away.

Composed 1966.

I was walking on the main road to Ise. The houses along the way had their shōji doors closed. The homes and the road were only one sheet of paper apart.

---

Season Word: *shōji*, "sliding door." Winter, life.

*Vocabulary:*
- *kaidō* is the traditional word for "highway"; though the word is seldom used in the names of new highways today, it remains in use in the names of many older highways.
- *shōji* refers to sliding doors that consist of a single layer of white paper pasted onto a wooden grid.
- *shimete* is the *-te* form of *shimeru* ("close/shut").
- *e* is a counter suffix for "layers," so *hitoe* means "one layer," and *kami hitoe* means "one sheet of paper."

218

佐鳴湖に　下りゐて鴨は　畝をなす

*Sanaruko ni　　ori ite kamo wa　　une o nasu*

## *On Sanaru Lake,*
## *a flock of ducks creating*
## *a field of furrows.*

Composed 1966.
Ducks have come down on Hamana Lake and on Sanaru Lake too.
They have ordered themselves into rows exactly like furrows in a
field. Duck furrows.

---

Season Word: *kamo*, "duck." Winter, animals.

*Vocabulary:*
- *-ko* is the suffix added to the names of lakes, so *Sanaruko* is "Lake Sanaru." It is
  a small lake near the much larger, and better known, Lake Hamana.
- *ori* is from *oriru* ("descend/land/alight").
- *ite* is the *-te* form of *iru*, which in classical Japanese often means "to sit." *Ori ite*
  = "alight and sit."
- *une* = "furrow(s)," and *nasu* = "make/form," so *une o nasu* = "form furrows."

大峯の　　そこには雪の　　紙を干す
Ōmine no　　soko ni wa yuki no　　kami o hosu

*Off on the summit*
*of Ōmine, snow paper*
*is spread out to dry.*

Composed 1967.
I had come to a paper mill in Yoshino, where white paper was drying.
Off in the interior of Yoshino, I could see Mount Ōmine under snow.
Mount Ōmine was drying snow paper.

Season Word: *kami o hosu*, "to dry paper." Winter, life.

*Vocabulary:*
- *soko* = "there," so *Ōmine no soko* is like "there in Ōmine."
- *yuki no kami* = "paper of snow/snow paper."
- *hosu* = "(hang/lay out to) dry"; Japanese paper is laid out to dry rather than hung.

歩かねば　ならぬ雪野を　人歩く

*Arukaneba*　　*naranu yukino o*　　*hito aruku*

# *Walking through the snow*
## *of a field he had no choice*
## *but to walk across.*

Composed 1967.
In the snow country, broad fields become snowy expanses, and there
is no way to get across them other than on foot. A man is walking
across one.

---

Season Word: *yuki*, "snow." Winter, celestial phenomena.

*Vocabulary:*
- *aruka-* is from *aruku* ("walk"), and *-neba naranu* is the classical equivalent of the
  verb ending *-nakereba naranai*, meaning "must/have to": *arukaneba naranu* =
  "must walk" → "have no choice but to walk." This phrase modifies *yukino* ("snowy
  field").
- *hito (wa/ga) aruku* = "a person/man walks."

雪嶺は　　はなびら鎌も　　御在所も
*Setsurei wa*　　*hanabira Kama mo*　　*Gozaisho mo*

# *The snowy peaks all —*
# *Gozaisho, the Sickle, too —*
# *become white petals.*

Composed 1967.

The Suzuka Mountains consist of seven peaks in a row, and yet each of these peaks stands alone. When snow gathers on them, the peaks look like white petals — Mount Kama, Mount Gozaisho, and the rest.

---

✦　Season Word: *setsurei*, "snowy peak." Winter, topography.

*Vocabulary:*
- *setsurei wa hanabira* is literally "the snowy peaks are flower petals."
- *Kama* (literally, "Sickle") and *Gozaisho* are the names of mountains (see page 155).
- *– mo – mo* means "both – and –."

巣燕も　　覚めゐて四時に　　竈を焚く

Sutsubame mo　　same-ite yoji ni　　kama o taku

## *Kindling a fire*
## *at 4 A. M., when only*
## *mother swallow stirs.*

Composed 1967.
In accordance with long-standing tradition, the wife of the owner of
the Akafuku store, in Ise, gets up at 4:00 A. M. and lights a fire.
Swallows are awake too at that time. The lady and the swallows in
the nest are the only ones awake.

---

✦　Season Word: *sutsubame*, "nesting swallow." Spring, animals.

*Vocabulary:*
- *su* = "nest," and *tsubame* = "swallow(s)," so *sutsubame* means "the swallows in their nests/nesting swallows."
- *mo* = "also."
- *same-ite* is an equivalent of modern *samete-ite* ("have awoken/are awake, and . . ."), from *(me ga) sameru*, "awaken."
- *yoji* = "4 o'clock," and *yoji ni* = "at 4 o'clock."
- *kama* = "kitchen stove/oven," and *taku* = "build/kindle a fire," so *kama o taku* is essentially "light the stove."

鮎に張る　　鶴翼の陣　　下り簗
*Ayu ni haru*　　*kakuyoku no jin*　　*kudari yana*

*Trap set for ayu,*
*a crane's-wings encirclement*
*extended downstream.*

Composed 1967.
The Ibi River is a stream for catching *ayu*. Trap nets are set to catch
the fish as they swim downstream. When I saw the trap net with its
wings spread, I was reminded of the military tactic known as the
"crane's-wing formation."

◆　Season Word: *kudari yana*, "downstream trap." Autumn, life.

*Vocabulary:*
- *ayu* is sometimes translated as "sweetfish."
- in association with a net or trap, *haru* means "spread/stretch/extend/set"; in asso-
  ciation with *jin* ("battle formation/position"), it means "set up/form/take up."

*Other points of interest:*
- the *kakuyoku no jin*, or "crane's-wings encirclement," is a famous military tactic,
  used by Takeda Shingen against Uesugi Kenshin in the battle of Kawanakajima
  in Nagano, in 1561. It is an arrangement of troops in an open V, designed to
  enclose the enemy on three sides.

224

枯洲より　　見る南面の　　福山城
*Karesu yori*　　*miru nanmen no*　　*Fukuyamajō*

## *Fukuyama Castle,*
## *viewed from the withered island*
## *facing its south wall.*

Composed 1967.
In front of Myōō-in Temple, in Fukuyama, is a great, reed-covered
sandbar. Off to the north looms the front of Fukuyama Castle. A
lucky castle, one that faces south.

---

✦　Season Word: *karesu*, "island of brown reeds." Winter, topography.

*Vocabulary:*
- *yori* = "from," and . . . *yori miru* = "view/viewed from . . ."
- *-jō* is the suffix added to the names of castles: *Fukuyamajō* = "Fukuyama Castle."
- *nanmen* is "south face," but here, *nanmen no* means *nanmen shite-iru*, "is facing south."
- *karesu yori miru* ("[I] viewed [it] from a withered island") can be thought of as modifying the combination *nanmen no Fukuyamajō* ("the south-facing Fukuyama Castle"). Or the poem can be viewed as a case of inverted syntax: *nanmen no Fukuyamajō (o) karesu yori miru* = "[I] view the south-facing Fukuyama Castle from a withered island."

225

春潮に　　飛島はみな　　子持島
*Shunchō ni*　　*Tobishima wa mina*　　*komochijima*

# *The spring tides arrive;*
# *all Tobishima islands*
# *have a child or more.*

Composed 1968.
Off the mouth of Ikenoura Cove, in Ise Bay, the islands known as the
Tobishimas stand in a row. Each island stands with a smaller com-
panion, a smaller island, like mother and child. When the spring tides
rise, the Tobishima isles ride like mothers and children.

---

✦　Season Word: *shunchō*, "spring tides." Spring, topography.

*Vocabulary:*
- *shunchō ni* = "in/on/amidst the spring tides."
- *mina* = "all."
- *ko* ("child") + *mochi* (from *motsu*, "to have/hold") + *jima* (from *shima*, "island")
  is essentially "island with child."

白面の　　皇后飾り　武者として

*Hakumen no　　kōgō kazari　　musha to shite*

## *Here is the Empress*
## *in white face, masquerading*
## *as a samurai.*

Composed 1968.

The Empress Jingō doll stands in a display among samurai dolls. Since she is wearing armor, she, too, is a samurai. Yet her powdered face is pure white. Dare we call the Empress in her powered face a samurai?

---

Season Word: *musha ningyō*, "samurai doll." Summer, observances.

*Vocabulary:*
- *hakumen* is literally "white face," so *hakumen no kōgō* = "Empress in/with white face."
- *kazari* is from *kazaru* ("display") and it modifies *musha* ("samurai"), so *kazari musha* means "displayed samurai" → "samurai doll."
- – *to shite* is an expression meaning "as –" → "as a samurai."

227

蜘蛛の囲に　かかり螢火　はや食はる

*Kumo no i ni*　　*kakari hotarubi*　　*haya kuwaru*

# *A firefly's light*
# *ensnared in a spider's web,*
# *swiftly devoured.*

Composed 1968.

I saw a spider web in a tree in a valley inhabited by fireflies. The light from a firefly became caught in the web, then darkened. The spider had devoured the firefly.

---

Season Word: *hotaru*, "firefly." Summer, animals.

*Vocabulary:*
- *kumo* = "spider," and *kumo no i* = "spider's web."
- *kakari* is from *kakaru*, "be snared/caught [in a trap/on a hook]."
- *hotarubi* = "firefly light."
- *haya* is a classical equivalent of *hayaku*, the adverb form of *hayai* ("fast/quick") → "quickly/swiftly."
- 食はる *kuwaru* is a classical equivalent of 食われる *kuwareru*, the passive form of 食う *kuu* ("eat") → "is eaten/devoured." *Hotarubi haya kuwaru* = "the firefly light is swiftly devoured."

火なき舟　沖に鯖火を　つけに行く
*Hi naki fune　　oki ni sababi o　　tsuke ni yuku*

## *Running in darkness,*
## *boat goes to mackerel grounds,*
## *then turns on its lamps.*

Composed 1968.
A boat leaving port on a mackerel-fishing trip. The departing boat is all dark. When it gets out in the open water, it turns on its mackerel-lights. The boat which until then was without lights becomes a mackerel-light boat.

---

Season Word: *saba,* "mackerel." Summer, animals.

*Vocabulary:*
- 火, read *hi* by itself and *-bi* in combinations, means "fire/light." *Sababi* = "mackerel lights."
- *naki* is the classical *-ki* form of *nai* ("not have"), for modifying nouns, so *hi naki fune* is "boat without light" → "boat (running) in darkness."
- *oki* = "the offing," and *oki ni (iku)* = "(go) out to sea."
- *tsuke* is from *tsukeru,* "light [a fire]/turn on [a light]."
- *yuku* is an alternate form of *iku* ("go"), and *ni yuku* after another verb means "go to do/go for the purpose of . . ." In this case, *tsuke ni yuku* means "go to light/turn on" in the sense that that is what they "will do" rather than that is their express purpose for going.

229

生きて吾　在り渦潮の　中にあり

*Ikite ware*　*ari uzushio no*　*naka ni ari*

### *Here in the middle*
### *of a swirling maelstrom,*
### *I know I exist.*

Composed 1968.
The tide-watching tourboat entered the whirlpool and circled with
it—an extraordinary place for a human being to be. There I became
acutely aware of my existence.

Season Word: *uzushio*, "whirlpool." Spring, topography.

*Vocabulary:*
- *ikite* is the *-te* form of *ikiru* ("to live").
- *ware* is a word for "I/me" in classical Japanese.
- *ari* is the classical "dictionary form" of *aru* ("exist[s]"). In classical times use of
  the word was not restricted to inanimate things. *Ware ari* = "I exist," and *uzushio
  no naka ni ari* = "[I] exist in a maelstrom."

熊の子が　　飼はれて鉄の　　鎖舐む
*Kuma no ko ga*　　*kawarete tetsu no*　　*kusari namu*


## *Nurtured in a cage,*
## *a bear cub licking away*
## *at his iron chain.*


Composed 1968.
Here is a bear caught in the interior of Mount Hakusan. He spends his
days in an iron cage, tied by an iron chain. He licks his iron chain,
the chain that restricts his freedom.

---

✦　Season Word: *kuma*, "bear." Winter, animals.

*Vocabulary:*
- *kuma no ko* is literally "child of bear" → "bear cub."
- *kawareta* is the *-te* form of *kawareru* ("be kept/nurtured as a pet"), from *kau* ("keep/ nurture as a pet").
- *tetsu no kusari* = "iron chain."
- *namu* is the classical form of *nameru* ("lick"). *O*, for direct object, has been omitted after *kusari*.

火に焚ける　　俵の裡に　　焔無し
*Hi ni takeru*　　*tawara no uchi ni*　　*honoo nashi*

## *A straw bag on fire*
## *with no flame penetrating*
## *its interior.*

Composed 1968.

I stood an empty straw bag on the ground and lighted it. It burned furiously. However, when I looked inside it, I could see no flames. Only the outside was burning.

---

Season Word: *hi ni takeru*, "to set on fire." Winter, life.

*Vocabulary:*
- *hi ni takeru* is a complete thought/sentence ("[I] set [it] on fire") modifying *tawara* ("straw bag"), and *hi ni takeru tawara* ("the straw bag that I set on fire") in turn modifies *uchi* ("the inside").
- *uchi ni* = "in the inside."
- *honoo* = "flames."
- *nashi* is the classical "dictionary form" of *nai* ("not exist/are none"), so *honoo nashi* = "there are no flames."

もがりぶえ　とぎれとぎれの　ものがたり

*Mogaribue*　　　*togire-togire no*　　　*monogatari*

***Wind over fences,***
***intoning by fits and starts***
***its old, old story.***

Composed 1968.
When wind strikes a slender object, it creates a sound. To listen to it,
one is apt to think that it is fitfully telling a story. This haiku is
entirely in hiragana.

---

Season Word: *mogaribue*, "wind whistle." Winter, celestial phenomena.

*Vocabulary:*
- *mogari* is a particular kind of bamboo fence, and *-bue* is from *fue* ("whistle"; *f* changes to *b* for euphony). *Mogaribue* refers to the sound of the winter wind whistling through/over a bamboo fence or any other object that vibrates/whistles in the wind.
- *togire* is from *togireru* ("break off/be interrupted"), and *togire-togire* describes something that proceeds "intermittently/with repeated interruptions/with stops and starts."
- *monogatari* = "tale/story," from *mono* ("thing[s]") and the noun form of *kataru* ("speak of/tell about"; *k* changes to *g* for euphony).

剛直の　冬の妙義を　引寄せる

*Gōchoku no    fuyu no Myōgi o      hikiyoseru*

*Incorruptible*
*Myōgi in winter — I draw*
*the mountain to me.*

Composed 1968.
Mount Myōgi can be viewed from the prospect at Karuizawa Pass. In the winter particularly, the mountain stands forth as upright and strong. As I look I draw it in my direction.

---

Season Word: *fuyu*, "winter." Winter, season.

*Vocabulary:*
- 剛 *gō* means "strong/hard/rigid," 直 *choku* means "straight/correct," and the combination refers to "integrity/uprightness." *Gōchoku no* modifies *fuyu no Myōgi* ("Mount Myōgi in winter").
- *hiki* is from *hiku* ("pull/draw"), and *yoseru* means "set/put/bring near (to)," so *hikiyoseru* is "draw toward me."

神懸を　　写し青嶺が　　石となる

*Kankake o*　　*utsushi aone ga*　　*ishi to naru*

*Kankake Valley —*
*green summits represented*
*in a stone garden.*

Composed 1968.
Eikō-ji Temple stands at the entrance to Kankakei Gorge, on the
island of Shōdo. There one can find a stone garden that is a model of
Kankakei Gorge. In midsummer, when the valley is pure green, its
representation is pure stone. Symbolism.

---

◆　Season Word: *aone*, "green summits." Summer, topography.

*Vocabulary:*
- 神懸 *Kankake* (or *Kamikake*) is the old name used for referring to the Kankakei Gorge area.
- *utsushi* is from *utsusu* ("copy/reflect [an image of]"). The implied subject is the stone garden Seishi mentions in his note: "The garden copies/reflects Kankake, and . . ."
- *ishi* = "stone/rock."
- . . . *to naru* means "becomes . . ." → *ishi to naru* = "become rocks/becomes a rock."

235

雛の饌　　落ちてあとより　　流れゆく
*Hina no sen*　　*ochite ato yori*　　*nagare yuku*

# *The food offering*
# *soon falls away from the dolls*
# *and floats behind them.*

Composed 1969.
The doll offering on the Chiyo River. Paper dolls were placed on
round straw plates, along with food offerings for them. The food fell
into the water very quickly, but it floated behind the dolls as they
were carried by the current.

Season Word: *hina*, "festival doll." Spring, observances.

*Vocabulary:*
- *ochite* is the *-te* form of *ochiru* ("fall"): "[it] falls, and . . ."
- *ato* = "behind/in back/after," and *yori* = "from," so *ato yori* = "from behind."
- *nagare* is from *nagareru* ("flow/be carried on a current"), and *yuku* means "go," so *nagare yuku* is like "goes flowing" → *ato kara nagare yuku* = "flows/floats behind/after."

*Other points of interest:*
- one of the ceremonies of the doll festival, held on March 3, is the *nagashibina*, or "doll floating," in which miniature paper dolls, and often dolls that have been played with, are set adrift on rivers or at sea to rid the children who made/owned them of evil spirits.

236

遠き世の　如く遠くに　蓮の華

*Tōki yo no*　　*gotoku tōku ni*　　*hasu no hana*

## *Lotus in distance —*
## *appearing as far away*
## *as a distant world.*

Composed 1969.

I went into Ritsurin Park by the back entrance and came to the pond just inside the gate. On the far side of the pond, lotuses were in bloom, looking like they were part of a Buddhist painting. They were lotuses in a far-off world.

---

Season Word: *hasu*, "lotus." Summer, plants.

*Vocabulary:*
- *tōki* is the classical *-ki* form of *tōi* ("distant/far away"); *tōki yo* = "distant world."
- *no gotoku* means "being/seeming like," so *tōki yo no gotoku* means "seeming like a distant world." This entire phrase modifies *tōku ni* ("in/at a far place" — *tōku* is a noun form of *tōi*): "in a far place seeming like a distant world."

*Other points of interest:*
- Ritsurin Park, in Takamatsu, Shikoku, is ranked among the top three of Japan's garden parks, a distinction it shares with the Kenrokuen of Kanazawa, and Kōrakuen of Okayama.

廻遊の　吾に万緑　蹤き来たる
*Kaiyū no　ware ni banryoku　tsuki kitaru*

***Following the route,***
***with a myriad of green leaves***
***not far behind me.***

Composed 1969.
I followed the route around the pond in Ritsurin Park. The park was filled with trees in green leaf. The green foliage followed me everywhere. All turned out to welcome me.

---

Season Word: *banryoku*, "green leaves season." Summer, plants.

*Vocabulary:*

- *kaiyū* refers to a "circular trip/tour," and *no* makes it a modifier for *ware* ("I/me"): *kaiyū no ware* = "I who am/was making a circular trip/tour."
- *tsuki kitaru* is an equivalent of modern *tsuite kita*, the *-te* form of *tsuku* ("stick/attach to") and the past form of *kuru* ("come") → "came following." *Ware ni tsuki kitaru* = "followed me."

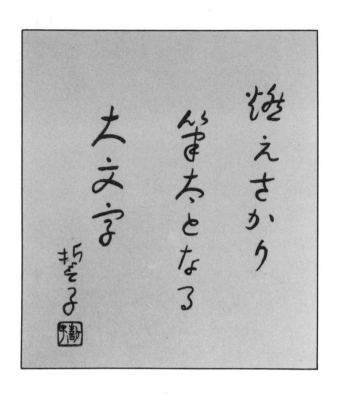

燃えさかり
筆太となる
大文字

哲子

燃えさかり　　筆太となる　　大文字
*Moesakari*　　*fudebuto to naru*　　*daimonji*

*Bonfire at its height,*
*the kanji "Great" is written*
*with a stubby brush.*

Composed 1969.
The festival of the character for "Great," in Kyōto. It is featured by a
tremendous bonfire to accompany the spirits of the dead. When the
burning begins, the character has the shape ordinarily given it by a
brush, but when the fire is at its height it has a swollen look, as if the
brush has lost its tip.

---

◆　Season Word: *daimonji*, "character for 'great'." Autumn, observances.

*Vocabulary:*
- *moe* is from *moeru* ("burn"), and *-sakari* is from *-sakaru*, a verb suffix implying
  the action reaches/is at its height. *Moesakari* = "the burning reaches its height,
  and . . ."
- *fude* = "writing brush," and *buto* is from *futoi* ("thick/fat"), so *fudebuto to naru* is
  literally "become thick-brushed" — referring to characters whose lines are fat
  and run together because the brush has lost its point.

*Other points of interest:*
- on August 16, as part of the Bon Festival, or "Festival of the Dead," a great fire
  describing the character 大, "great," is set on Daimonjiyama ("Great Character
  Mountain") facing Kyōto.

み仏の　　　肩に秋日の　　　手が置かれ

Mihotoke no　　kata ni akibi no　　te ga okare

# The sun of autumn
# rests its hand on the shoulder
# of holy Buddha.

Composed 1969.

A Buddha image is carved into a cliff above Kizetsu Canyon, in Kii Tanabe. Rays of the setting sun of autumn shine on His shoulder. That sunbeam looks like the hand of the Dainichi Buddha. His hand has been placed on the shoulder of this Buddha.

---

◆　Season Word: *akibi*, "autumn sun." Autumn, celestial phenomena.

*Vocabulary:*
- *mi-* is an honorific prefix, like *o-*.
- *hotoke* = "Buddha (image)," and *hotoke no kata* = "shoulder of the Buddha (image)."
- *akibi no te* = "autumn sun's hand."
- *okare* implies *okarete-iru* ("is set/placed [upon]"), a passive form of *oku* ("set/ place").

芭蕉忌に　ビルのガラスの　絶壁よ

*Bashōki ni*　　　*biru no garasu no*　　　*zeppeki yo*

## *Day to remember*
## *Bashō — wall of a building,*
## *precipice of glass.*

Composed 1969.
Bashō died near Minami Midō, in Ōsaka. I attended the memorial service for Bashō and glimpsed the glass wall of the C. Itoh Building towering off to the north. It was a precipice of glass, something unknown to Bashō.

---

Season Word: *Bashōki*, "anniversary of Bashō's death." Winter, observances.

*Vocabulary:*
- *Bashōki* can refer either to the anniversary of Bashō's death or to memorial services held on that day.
- *biru no garasu no zeppeki* = "a precipice formed by the glass of a (tall) building."
- *yo* is exclamatory.

涅槃図に　継ぎ目涅槃を　継ぎ合はす

*Nehanzu ni　　tsugime nehan o　　tsugiawasu*

## *The Nirvana scroll —*
## *Nirvana is whole again*
## *even in its seams.*

Composed 1969.

The Jakushō-ji was the temple of the painter-priest Gessen. On the anniversary of the Buddha's death, they hang an old nirvana scroll, with repair-cracks running down its length. Thus the image of Buddha in nirvana is reconstituted.

---

Season Word: *nehanzu*, "nirvana scroll." Spring, observances.

*Vocabulary:*
- *nehan* = "nirvana," and *nehanzu* = "nirvana scroll."
- *tsugi-* is from *tsugu* ("to patch"), and *-me* is added to certain verbs to refer to the point where the action took place/was done, so *tsugime* = "patched seam/repaired crack."
- *nehanzu ni tsugime* implies . . . *ga aru* : "there is a patched seam in the nirvana scroll."
- *tsugiawasu* means "patch together," so *nehan o tsugiawasu* literally means "patch nirvana together."

244

天高く　　遠流の遠を　　飛びて来し

Ten takaku　　onru no on o　　tobite kishi

*High in the heavens,*
*I have flown the length over*
*of the exile's sail.*

Composed 1969.
I flew from Izumo to Oki Island. Long ago Oki Island was a place of exile, and exiles were taken there by boat. The long journey there I negotiated by plane.

---

Season Word: *ten takaku*, "high in the sky." Autumn, celestial phenomena.

*Vocabulary:*
- *ten takaku* ("high in the sky") is an adverb phrase modifying *tobite kishi*, which is equivalent to modern *tonde kita* ("[I] came flying").
- *onru* is a word for "exile" combining the kanji for "far/distant" and "wash away/set adrift."
- *on o tobite kishi* is a play on the first kanji of *onru*, something like saying, "I came flying the 'far' of 'far exile'" → "I came flying the full length of the exiles' journey."

*Other points of interest:*
- the Oki Islands, 40-50 miles off the coast of Honshū, in Shimane Prefecture, were home to high-ranking exiles, including Emperor Go-Daigo (1288-1339).

初凪に　　岬燈台　　白一指
*Hatsunagi ni　　misaki tōdai　　shiro isshi*

# *In the New Year's calm,*
# *the lighthouse upon the cape*
# *is a white finger.*

Composed 1970.

The sea rested peacefully in the New Year's calm. On that sea a cape stood out, with a white lighthouse on its tip. The white lighthouse looked like a finger — a white finger on the sea in the calm of the New Year.

---

Season Word: *hatsunagi*, "New Year's calm." New Year's, celestial phenomena.

*Vocabulary:*
- *misaki* = "cape/promontory/headland."
- *tōdai* = "lighthouse."
- *shiro* = "white," and *isshi* = "one finger," so *shiro isshi* = "a single white finger."

桜咲く　　前より紅気　立ちこめて
*Sakura saku*　　*mae yori kōki*　*tachikomete*

***Just before they bloom,***
***the cherry blossom branches***
***have a sense of pink.***

Composed 1970.
I looked at cherry branches before the blossoms came out. The branches were enveloped in a pink haze. That pink haze is the harbinger of the pink of the blossoms. It reveals itself.

Season Word: *sakura*, "cherry blossom." Spring, plants.

*Vocabulary:*
- *saku* = "to bloom/blossom."
- *sakura saku* is a complete thought/sentence ("cherry blossoms bloom") modifying *mae* ("before"): "before the cherry blossoms bloom."
- *yori* = "from," and . . . *mae yori* = "from before . . ."
- 紅 *kō* is "red/crimson," and 気 *ki* is "air/ether/aura" → "pink haze."
- *tachikomete* is from *tachikomeru*, which means "envelop/shroud/hang over" when speaking of haze/mist/smoke/etc.

247

九頭龍の　　谷残雪も　　多頭龍

*Kuzuryū no　　tani zansetsu mo　　tatōryū*

## *Even the snow piles*
## *left in Nine-head Dragon glen*
## *are many-headed.*

Composed 1970.
The Nine-head Dragon is at Hakusan Shrine. When I went upstream
along the Nine-head Dragon River, I thought the snow lingering in
the valley had the shape of a dragon with many heads.

✦　Season Word: *zansetsu*, "remaining snow." Spring, topography.

*Vocabulary:*
- *kuzuryū* means "nine-headed dragon" and *tatōryū* means "many-headed dragon."
- *tani* = "valley/glen"; *Kuzuryū no tani* = "Nine-headed Dragon Glen."
- *mo* = "even/also," so *zansetsu mo* = "even the remaining/lingering snow."
- *da/desu* ("is") is implied at the end: "even the remaining snow is/looks like a many-headed dragon."

龍宮の　　門南風を　　奉る
*Ryūgū no*　　*mon nanpū o*　　*tatematsuru*

# *The Dragon Hall Gate —*
# *the south wind is ushered in*
# *as an offering.*

Composed 1970.
The Akama Shrine, in Shimonoseki, has a red gate, known as the Dragon Hall Gate. The south wind comes off the sea, passes through the Dragon Hall Gate, and reaches the spirit of the Infant Emperor, to whom the Main Hall is dedicated. The shrine brings the south wind through the Dragon Hall Gate as an offering.

---

✦　Season Word: *nanpū*, "south wind." Summer, celestial phenomena.

*Vocabulary:*
- 宮 *gū* (or *miya*) can refer to a "palace" or "shrine," or to a particular part of a palace or shrine ("hall"). *Ryūgū* = "Dragon Palace/Hall," and *Ryūgū no Mon* = "Dragon Hall Gate."
- *tatematsuru*, meaning "give/present/offer up," is a humble verb, which shows respect by humbling the giver and elevating the receiver.
- supplying the particle *ga*, for subject, after *mon*, the poem could mean "The Dragon Hall Gate offers up the south wind," but Seishi's note explains it as "The south wind is offered up through the Dragon Hall Gate."

249

ひぐらしが　　下界に鳴けり　　皇子のため

*Higurashi ga*　　*gekai ni nakeri*　　*miko no tame*

## *Clear cicada song*
## *echoing about the earth*
## *in prayer for the prince.*

Composed 1970.
The Kachio Temple, in Minoo. On top of the mountain is the grave of
Prince Kaijō. When I went up the mountain and visited the grave, I
heard the voice of an evening cicada in the temple trees — a prayer
for the prince's soul.

---

◆　Season Word: *higurashi*, "clear cicada." Autumn, animals.

*Vocabulary:*
- *gekai* ("lower realm/lower state of existence") is a Buddhist word referring to "this world/the human world."
- *nakeri* is a classical equivalent of *naite-iru* ("is crying," from *naku*, "[an animal] cries/sings/calls").
- *miko* = "prince," and *miko no tame* = "for the prince."

250

透明の　氷塊四つの　部屋に伐る

*Tōmei no*　*hyōkai yotsu no*　*heya ni kiru*

## *Iceman with his saw*
## *cutting a clear block of ice*
## *into four chambers.*

Composed 1970.
An iceman carries a block of ice and places it on the ground. The block is transparent and marked into four quarters. The iceman takes his saw and cuts the block into four rooms.

---

Season Word: *hyōkai*, "block of ice" ("summer ice" implied). Summer, life.

*Vocabulary:*
- *tōmei* = "transparent."
- *hyōkai* is made up of the kanji for "ice" and "chunk/lump/clump" → "ice block."
- *yotsu* is the same as *yottsu*, the general purpose counter for "four"; *yotsu no heya* = "four rooms."
- *kiru* = "cut," and . . . *ni kiru* = "cut into . . ."

秋祭　　鬼面をかぶり　　心も鬼
*Akimatsuri*　　*kimen o kaburi*　　*kokoro mo oni*

# *Autumn festival —*
# *putting on a devil mask,*
# *devil to the core.*

Composed 1970.
At the Tenjin Festival at Ueno, in Iga, which has a connection with
Bashō, a devil leads the procession. In his mask, he is frightful to
look at. The man who plays the devil makes himself devilish at heart
and projects a devilish aura.

---

Season Word: *akimatsuri*, "autumn festival." Autumn, observances.

*Vocabulary:*
- 鬼, read *oni* by itself and *ki* in combinations, refers to a devilish/demonic figure, usually depicted with red face and horns: "devil/demon/ogre."
- 面 *men*, often meaning "face/surface," can also mean "mask." *Kimen* = "devil/ogre mask."
- *kaburi* is from *kaburu*, meaning "wear/put on" for things that cover or are pulled over the head. *Kimen o kaburi* = "he has put on a devil mask and . . ."

*Other points of interest:*
- Ueno is the castle town where Bashō grew up. It is unknown whether he was born there or born nearby shortly before his family moved there.

252

湯豆腐が　　煮ゆ角々が　　揺れ動き
*Yudōfu ga*　　*niyu kadokado ga*　　*yure ugoki*

## *Tōfu simmering —*
## *corner by corner trembling,*
## *shaking with the heat.*

Composed 1970.
Tōfu cooking in a pot on the gas burner. The cakes of tōfu shake at the corners in the hot water. Their shaking tells us the water is very hot.

---

Season Word: *yudōfu,* "simmered bean curd." Winter, life.

*Vocabulary:*
- *yu* = "hot water," and *-dōfu* is from *tōfu* ("tofu/bean curd"; *t* changes to *d* for euphony). *Yudōfu* is a popular cold-weather dish in which blocks of tofu are warmed in simmering water and eaten with a dipping sauce.
- *niyu* is equivalent to *nieru* ("simmer/boil") in modern Japanese.
- *kado* = "corner," and *kadokado* = "corners." 々 repeats the previous kanji.
- *yure* is from *yureru* ("shake/tremble/sway"), and *ugoki* is from *ugoku* ("to move"). The poem is in inverted syntax. Normal syntax would be *kadokado ga yure ugoki, yudōfu ga niyu,* "the corners shake and the tofu simmers" → "the tofu simmers with its corners shaking."

253

草の絮　　優遊富士の　　大斜面
*Kusa no wata*　　*yūyū Fuji no*　　*daishamen*

***Weed down descending***
***luxuriously over***
***Fuji's great incline.***

Composed 1970.
Standing high on the sandy terrain of Mount Fuji, I saw weed seeds
flying down its great slopes. They came down from grassy areas and
floated languidly before me.

---

Season Word: *kusa no wata*, "weed down." Autumn, plants.

*Vocabulary:*
- *kusa* = "grass/herb/weed."
- *wata* refers to the "down" that surrounds the seeds of many plants.
- *yūyū* combines the kanji for "gentle/graceful" and "play/be idle/wander."
- *dai-* is prefixed to kanji compounds to give the meaning "great –."
- *shamen* means "inclined surface," so *Fuji no daishamen* means "Fuji's great incline."

下界まで　断崖富士の　壁に立つ
*Gekai made　　dangai Fuji no　　kabe ni tatsu*

## *Standing at the top*
## *of the precipitous drop*
## *of Mount Fuji's wall.*

Composed 1970.
The top of Mount Fuji. When one looks from there down the mountain path, one sees a sharp descent all the way to the bottom. Fuji is surrounded by four sheer walls, and someone standing on its summit is at the apex of them.

---

✦　Season Word: *tozan*, "mountain climbing" (implied). Summer, life.

*Vocabulary:*
- *gekai* = "the world below."
- *made* = "to/as far as," and in this case *gekai made* means essentially "to the bottom (of the mountain)."
- *dangai* = "cliff/precipice"; *gekai made dangai* = "[it is] a precipice to the bottom."
- *kabe* = "wall," and *kabe ni tatsu* = "stand on/at the top of [Fuji's] wall."

青牧の　　柵開けて入り　　出でて閉む
Aomaki no　　saku akete iri　　idete shimu

*Green pasture gateway,*
*opening as I go in,*
*closing as I leave.*

Composed 1971.
Cattle are raised in a green pasture on a mountain on Hachijō Island.
I went through that pasture in a car. We opened the gate and went in,
and closed the gate when we came out.

---

Season Word: *aomaki*, "green pasture." Summer, topography.

*Vocabulary:*
- 青 *ao* here means "green," and *maki* stands for *makiba* ("pasture/grazing land").
- *saku* strictly speaking means "fence," but here must be thought of as "gate."
- *akete* is the *-te* form of *akeru* ("open"), and *iri* is the classical equivalent of *hairi* (from *hairu*, "enter/go in"), so *akete iri* is literally "open and enter."
- *idete* is the *-te* form of the classical verb *izu*, equivalent to modern *deru* ("exit/go out"), and *shimu* is the classical equivalent of *shimeru* ("close/shut"), so *idete shimu* is literally "exit and close."

三角を　　忌まずげんげの　　三角田
*Sankaku o*　　*imazu genge no*　　*sankakuda*

*A triangular*
　　*milk-vetch field that doesn't mind*
　　　*the triangular.*

Composed 1971.
It is a triangular field, beautiful because of the milk-vetch growing in
it. Being a three-cornered field may seem to give it bad luck, but just
as it was once a three-cornered rice field, it is now a three-cornered
milk-vetch field.

---

Season Word: *genge*, "milk vetch." Spring, plants.

*Vocabulary:*
- *sankaku* is literally "three corners" → "triangle."
- *imazu* is the classical negative form of *imu* ("hate/abhor/treat as taboo").
- 田 *ta* (in combinations read *-da* for euphony) refers specifically to "rice paddies/
  fields" rather than any other kind of field; *sankakuda* = "triangular paddy/field."

著莪の花　　帝の怨霊　　斑となりて

*Shaga no hana　　mikado no onryō　　fu to narite*

# *The Emperor's ghost*
# *is abroad in the speckling*
# *of this iris bloom.*

Composed 1971.

An iris was in bloom at the Shiramine Mausoleum, in Sanuki. When I saw the purple spots in that flower, I wondered if the vengeful spirit of the Emperor had coalesced in them.

---

Season Word: *shaga,* "iris." Summer, plants.

*Vocabulary:*
- *mikado* = "emperor."
- *onryō* = "vengeful spirit"; this is the subject of *fu to narite.*
- *fu* = "spot/speck/speckle," and *... to narite* is the classical *-te* form of *... to naru,* "becomes ...," so *fu to narite* means "becomes/became spots." Here this implies "has appeared/manifested itself as spots."

*Other points of interest:*
- the Shiramine Mausoleum is that of Emperor Sutoku (1119–64; r. 1123–41), who was forced by his father, ex-Emperor Toba, to abdicate the throne at a young age, and was later exiled when his faction at court failed in an effort to seize power after the death of his father.

ナイターの　　底下界にて　　最も明

*Naitā no*　　*soko gekai nite*　　*mottomo mei*

# *The very bottom*
## *of a night game, the brightest*
## *place under the sun.*

Composed 1971.
During a night game, I looked down at the field from my stadium
seat. The field was illuminated by dazzling lights. I thought it must
be the brightest place in the world.

---

Season Word: *naitā*, "night baseball game." Summer, life.

*Vocabulary:*
- *soko* refers to the "bottom" of a bowl/vessel/container.
- *gekai* = "lower realm" → "this world."
- *nite* = "at/in."
- *mottomo* = "most," and *mei* = "bright," so *mottomo mei* = "brightest."

観音の　　千手を今年　　竹も持つ

*Kannon no　　senju o kotoshi　　–dake mo motsu*

## *This year's bamboo, too,*
## *in the manner of Kannon,*
## *has a thousand hands.*

Composed 1971.
Above the Kinosaki hotspring is the Hotspring Temple. Here, where
an image of the Thousand-handed Kannon is enshrined, new bamboo
stalks extend countless branches. The new bamboo, too, has
Kannon's thousand hands.

---

◆　Season Word: *kotoshidake*, "this year's bamboo." Summer, plants.

*Vocabulary:*
- *Kannon* is the Buddhist god/goddess of mercy and compassion, who is often
  thought of as having a thousand arms/hands. Images of Kannon with many hands
  are called *Senju Kannon* (*senju* is literally "thousand arms/hands") — though
  they usually actually have only about 40 hands.
- *Kannon no senju* = "the thousand hands of Kannon"; this is the object of *motsu*,
  in the last line.
- *mo* = "also/too," and *motsu* = "have/possess" → *kotoshidake mo motsu* = "this
  year's bamboo also has [them]."

260

十里飛び　来て山頂に　蠅とまる

*Jūri tobi*　　　*kite sanchō ni*　　　*hae tomaru*

## A fly that has come
## mile upon mile and rested
## on this mountaintop.

Composed 1971.
I climbed Mount Fuji for the second time. When I stood at the top, a
fly came and landed on the ground, then on my hand. That fly had
come the ten leagues from the bottom of the mountain to light on me
and Fuji's summit.

---

Season Word: *hae,* "fly." Summer, animals.

*Vocabulary:*
- *ri* is an old unit of measure for distance, measuring about 2.5 miles or 4 kilometers. That would make *jūri* about 25 miles, but a precise measure is probably not intended here → "many miles/mile upon mile."
- *tobi kite* is equivalent to modern Japanese *tonde kite*, from *tobu* ("to fly") and *kuru* ("come") → "come/came flying and . . ."
- *sanchō* = "summit," and *sanchō ni* = "on the summit."
- *tomaru* = "stop," or in the case of an insect, "land/alight."

261

山に崎　　ありて摂津の　　国霞む
*Yama ni saki*　　*arite Settsu no*　　*kuni kasumu*

## Mountains can have capes;
## and the province of Settsu
## is covered with haze.

Composed 1972.
The place called Yamazaki is on one of the capes formed by the jagged
edge of a mountain. Mountains, too, have capes. The province of
Settsu, where Yamazaki is located, is now under haze. The mountain
cape is faintly visible in the haze.

---

✦　Season Word: *kasumu*, "become hazy." Spring, celestial phenomena.

*Vocabulary:*
- *saki* = "cape/promontory/headland." The name Yamazaki is written 山崎, liter-
  ally "mountain" + "cape" (*saki* changes to *zaki* for euphony), so the poem is
  partly a play on words.
- *arite* is the *-te* form of classical *ari*, which is equivalent to modern *aru* ("to
  have"); *yama ni saki arite* = "mountains have capes."
- *kuni* = "province," so *Settsu no kuni* = "the province of Settsu." The old Settsu
  spanned parts of modern Hyōgo and Ōsaka prefectures.
- *kasumi* is "haze," and *kasumu* means "become hazy."

早苗投ぐ　　青の塊　　飛んでゆく

*Sanae nagu*　　*ao no katamari*　　*tonde yuku*

## *A sheaf of rice sprouts*
## *flying into the rice field*
## *in a verdant lump.*

Composed 1972.
I was invited to cast sheaves of rice-seedlings on the rice fields of a
temple in Harima. In flight, each sheaf of seedlings looked like a green
clod. It landed upright in the wet field, in a shower of spray.

---

Season Word: *sanae*, "rice seedlings." Summer, plants.

*Vocabulary:*
- *nagu* is the classical form of *nageru* ("throw/toss").
- *katamari* = "clump/clod/chunk."
- *tonde* is the *-te* form of *tobu* ("fly") and *yuku* is an alternate form of *iku* ("go").
  *Iku* after the *-te* form of a verb indicates the action moves away from the
  speaker: "goes flying."

衆のため　　人師の使　　道をしへ
*Shū no tame*　　*daishi no tsukai*　　*michioshie*

## *"Way-teacher" beetle,*
## *a messenger to mankind*
## *from the great teacher.*

Composed 1972.
I paid a visit to the Temple of the Great Teacher, in Niu. When I went
up the stone stairs in front of the bell pavilion, a tiger beetle, waiting
for me, led me to the main hall, where the image of the Great Teacher
is enshrined. He did this not only for me, but for all mankind.

---

◆　Season Word: *michioshie*, "way-teacher beetle." Summer, animals.

*Vocabulary:*
- *shū* means "large number/mass of people" → "all humanity/everyone."
- *– no tame* = "for/for the sake of."
- *Daishi* (lit. "great teacher") refers to 弘法大師 *Kōbō Daishi*, better known to some as *Kūkai* (774-835), founder of the Shingon sect of Buddhism in Japan.
- *tsukai* (a noun form of *tsukau*, "use") means "messenger/emissary/servant."
- 道をしへ is the old spelling of 道おしえ *michioshie*, the Japanese name for "tiger beetle," which combines words meaning "road/path/way" and "tell/teach." The tiger beetle gained this name because it is known for flying ahead of pedestrians as if leading them. Thus, the last line implies, "the way-teacher beetle shows/ showed (me) the way."

# 高稲架に　潜り門あり　稲毛門
*Takahaza ni　　kugurimon ari　　inagemon*


# In the high rice frame,
### a gate one stoops to pass through —
### a low gate of rice.


Composed 1972.

On a farm by the Japan Sea on the Noto Peninsula, rice hanging to dry on a tall rice frame formed a windbreak. A gate had been fashioned in the lower part of the frame, and everyone ducked through it coming and going. It was a rice gate, a gate of rice ears.

---

Season Word: *haza*, "rice frame." Autumn, life.

*Vocabulary:*
- *taka-* is the prefix form of *takai* ("high/tall"); *haza* (or *hasa*), written with the kanji for "rice plant(s)" and "hang up/mount," refers to the frames on which harvested rice sheaves are hung up to dry.
- *kuguri* is from *kuguru* ("go under"), and *kugurimon* refers to a small gate that requires one to duck down/stoop low in order to pass through.
- *ari* is the classical form of *aru* ("have/exists/there is"): *kugurimon ari* = "there is a stoop gate."
- *inage* combines the words for "rice plant(s)" and "hair" to suggest "rice straw" → *inagemon* = "rice-straw gate."

聖夜餐　スープ平らに　搬び来し
*Seiyasan*　*sūpu taira-ni*　*hakobi kishi*

## *For Christmas dinner, soup is brought to the table on a level plane.*

Composed 1972.
Christmas dinner. Soup was brought to the table first. The waiter
exercised care to keep the soup bowls level. A worshipful Christmas
dinner.

---

Season Word: *seiya*, "Christmas Eve." Winter, observances.

*Vocabulary:*
- *seiya* is "Christmas Eve," so *seiyasan* is in fact "Christmas Eve dinner." Japanese celebrations of Christmas tend to focus more on Christmas Eve than on Christmas Day.
- *taira-ni* is an adverb meaning "level/in a level manner."
- *hakobi kishi* is equivalent to modern *hakonde kita*, the *-te* form of *hokobu* ("carry/transport") and the past form of *kuru* ("come") → "came carrying."

海峡の　　中道烏賊灯　　連なれり
*Kaikyō no　　nakamichi ikabi　　tsuranareri*

## *Road down the middle*
## *of the strait; a succession*
## *of cuttlefish lights.*

Composed 1972.

I flew over the Tsugaru Strait in a plane. Lamps were visible here and there on a road through the strait. They were cuttlefish lights, part of the hunt for cuttlefish in the strait.

---

Season Word: *ika*, "cuttlefish." Summer, animals.

*Vocabulary:*
- *kaikyō*, which combines the kanji for "sea" and "narrow," means "(sea) strait/ channel."
- *nakamichi* = "road running to/in/through the middle."
- *ikabi* is literally "squid/cuttlefish light" → "squid/cuttlefish boat lights."
- *tsuranareri* is a classical equivalent of *tsuranatte-iru* ("to be in a long line/row," from *tsuranaru*, "stretch/string out in a line").

御遷宮　万代守護の　　白鳥座
Gosengū　　bandai shugo no　　Hakuchōza

*Moving the great shrine —*
*under the eternal eye*
*of the Cygnus stars.*

Composed 1972.

I was able to assist in the transfer of the Ise Shrine by supervising the
kindling of the fire in the Inner Shrine. In the sky, the swan constella-
tion had spread its wings, the same stars I saw when I helped with the
last transfer. They are the stars of eternal protection.

---

Season Word: *gosengū*, "moving the Great Shrine." Autumn, observances.

*Vocabulary:*
- *go-* is an honorific prefix, and *sengū* refers to the moving of a shrine.
- *bandai* is literally "ten-thousand ages" → "all ages/eternity."
- *shugo* = "protection/protector."
- *hakuchō* is literally "white bird" → "swan," and *-za* is the suffix for "constella-
tion," so *Hakuchōza* = "swan constellation" → "Cygnus."

*Other points of interest:*
- the Inner Shrine of the Great Shrine at Ise is rebuilt and moved back and forth
between adjoining lots every twenty years.

切通し　多羅尾寒風　押し通る
*Kiridōshi*　　*Tarao kampū*　　*oshi tōru*

*Narrow mountain pass*
*with the cold Tarao wind*
*forcing its way through.*

Composed 1972.
Whenever Bashō went to Kyōto from Ueno, in Iga, he crossed the
Otogi Pass to Tarao. When I went that way, the cold wind from Tarao
came barreling through the pass.

---

✦　Season Word: *kanpū*, "cold wind." Winter, celestial phenomena.

*Vocabulary:*
- *kiri* is from *kiru* ("cut"), and *-dōshi* is from *tōru* ("go/pass through"; *t* changes to *d* for euphony); *kiridōshi* refers to a place where an opening/hollow has been cut in a hill/mountain for the road to pass through.
- *Tarao* is a place name, and *kanpū* means "cold wind," so *Tarao kanpū* is "the cold wind of/from Tarao."
- *oshi* (from *osu*, "push") plus *tōru* make a work meaning "push through" → "force [its way] through." The subject of this verb is "cold wind."

絨緞を　　敷きて冷えきる　　天守閣
*Jūtan o*　　*shikite hiekiru*　　*tenshukaku*

# *The castle sanctum —*
# *even under a carpet*
# *still as cold as ice.*

Composed 1972.
I climbed to the tower sanctum of Inuyama Castle. The room was
extremely cold. A carpet had been spread on the floor, but it did
nothing to warm the place. Even with the carpet it was cold.

---

Season Word: *jūtan*, "carpet." Winter, life.

*Vocabulary:*
- *shikite* is the old *-te* form of *shiku*, which means to "lay/spread/put down." Here the *-te* form implies *-te mo*, "even if/even with," so *jūtan o shikite* = "even with a carpet spread."
- *hie* is the stem form of *hieru*, "become chilled," and *-kiru* after the stem of another verb implies "completely/to the greatest extent possible."
- *tenshukaku* = "keep/castle sanctum" — see poem 43.

げんげ田の　　広大これが　　美濃の国
*Gengeda no*　　*kōdai kore ga*　　*Mino no kuni*

*Where the milk-vetch fields*
*become broad plains, there you have*
*the land of Mino.*

Composed 1972.
Mino province is given over to fields of milk vetch. The milk-vetch
fields *are* Mino. As you go deep into the province, the milk-vetch
fields get broader. Those broad milk-vetch fields are Mino.

---

✦　Season Word: *genge*, "milk vetch." Spring, plants.

*Vocabulary:*
- 田 -*da* (or *ta* when standing alone) usually refers to rice paddies/fields but is also used in *gengeda*, "milk-vetch fields," because milk-vetch is often planted as a second crop in dry rice paddies/fields.
- *kōdai* combines the kanji for "wide/spacious" and "big" → "broad/broadness."
- *kore* means "this," and *kore ga* . . . implies *da/desu* ("is/are") at the end: "This is/ these are . . ."
- *kuni* = "land/province," so *Mino no kuni* = "the province of Mino." Mino was the southern part of today's Gifu Prefecture.

逆立ちて　金魚艶なる　姿見す

*Sakadachite*　*kingyo en naru*　*sugata misu*

# Standing on its head
# the shape the goldfish shows off
# has a certain charm.

Composed 1972.
I watched a goldfish in a tank as it stood on its head with its tail bent over and its fins hanging loosely at its sides. It was rather fetching in its disheveled state.

---

Season Word: *kingyo*, "goldfish." Summer, animals.

*Vocabulary:*
- *sakadachite* is the old *-te* form of *sakadatsu*, meaning "stand on end/stand on one's head."
- *en* = "charm," and *en naru* is a classical equivalent of *en-na*, "charming/fascinating/bewitching/captivating." This modifies *sugata*, "shape/figure," to give the meaning "charming shape/figure."
- *misu* is the classical equivalent of *miseru* ("show/display"), so *sakadachite . . . misu* means "stands on its head and shows . . ." The subject is "goldfish," and the object is "charming shape/figure."

272

要塞に　生き殘るもの　蜥蜴のみ

*Yōsai ni　　ikinokoru mono　　tokage nomi*

## *Island of bunkers —*
## *the only thing remaining,*
## *the lizards alone.*

Composed 1972.
The fortified island of Kada, at the mouth of Ōsaka Bay. The fortress
is vacant except for lizards. The only living things still there are
lizards. When people come by, they tremble.

---

Season Word: *tokage*, "lizard." Summer, animals.

*Vocabulary:*
- *yōsai* = "fortress/stronghold"; *yōsai ni* = "at the fortress."
- *ikinokoru*, from *ikiru* ("live") and *nokoru* ("remain"), means "remain living/survive." *Yōsai ni ikinokoru* is a complete thought/sentence ("remain living at the fortress") modifying *mono* ("thing," or, in this case, "creature").
- *nomi* = "only."

273

白き背を　吾に向けたる　　雲の峯
*Shiroki se o*　　*ware ni muketaru*　　*kumo no mine*

## *Cloud promontories*
## *giving me no view except*
## *their white shoulder blades.*

Composed 1972.

I looked out from the fortified island and saw a gigantic column of clouds standing above the mountains. White cloud peaks showed me their white backs. They were ignoring me. I wondered if they were sulking.

---

Season Word: *kumo no mine*, "cumulus clouds." Summer, celestial phenomena.

*Vocabulary:*
- *shiroki* is the classical *-ki* form of *shiroi* ("white"), modifying *se* ("back").
- *ware* means "I/me" in classical Japanese.
- *muketaru* is a classical equivalent of *mukete-iru*, the progressive form of *mukeru* ("turn one's face/back/side toward").
- *kumo* = "clouds," and *mine* = "peak/mountain," so *kumo no mine* literally means "peak/mountain of clouds" → "a great column/tower/bank of (cumulus) clouds."
- *shiroki se o ware ni muketaru* is a complete thought/sentence ("[it] turns [its] white back toward me") modifying *kumo no mine*.

274

星よりも　　　明螢火の　　　生ける火は
*Hoshi yori mo*　　　*mei hotarubi no*　　　*ikeru hi wa*

## *The living fire*
## *of a firefly glowing*
## *brighter than a star.*

Composed 1972.
A firefly hunt in a valley deep in Takatsuki. A firefly flashed in the air above the valley. Stars were out, but the firefly's light was much brighter. That is because the firefly is living fire.

---

Season Word: *hotaru*, "firefly." Summer, animals.

*Vocabulary:*
- *hoshi* = "star(s)."
- . . . *yori mo* = "more than/even more than . . ."
- *mei* = "bright"; *hoshi yori mo mei* = "brighter than a star."
- *hotarubi* = "firefly light."
- *ikeru* is a classical equivalent of *ikite-iru* ("is alive/living," from *ikiru*, "to live"), which modifies *hi* ("fire"): *ikeru hi* = "living fire."
- *hotarubi no ikeru hi wa* means "The living fire of the firefly's light . . ." Inverted syntax then takes the reader back to the beginning of the poem: ". . . is brighter than a star."

水神に　　守られ冬も　　大河なり
*Suijin ni*　　*mamorare fuyu mo*　　*taiga nari*

# By the water god
# protected, a great river
# even in winter.

Composed 1972.

The Sumiyoshi Shrine juts out over the Ibi River, in Kuwana. One wintry day, I looked at the river from the stone shrine staircase that faces it. Even in winter, it is a broad, deep river. Sumiyoshi is the god of water and protects the shrine.

---

◆ Season Word: *fuyu*, "winter." Winter, season.

*Vocabulary:*
- *suijin* is literally "water god."
- *mamorare* is from *mamorareru* ("is protected"), the passive form of *mamoru* ("protect"); . . . *ni mamorare* = "is protected by . . ."
- *fuyu mo* = "in winter, too/even in winter."
- *taiga* = "great river," and *nari* is a classical equivalent of *da/desu* ("is").

大雪が　　押す禅堂の　　雪囲ひ

*Ōyuki ga*　　*osu zendō no*　　*yukigakoi*

*Barriers that guard*
*this Zen hall against the snows,*
*under their pressure.*

Composed 1972.
Eihei-ji under snow. When I visited the Jōyō Hall, sacred to the memory of the priest Dōgen, it was surrounded by snow fences. Heavy snow pressed against the fences, bending them over.

---

Season Word: *ōyuki*, "heavy snow." Winter, celestial phenomena.

*Vocabulary:*
- *ō-* is the prefix form of *ōkii* ("large/great"); *ōyuki* = "great/heavy/deep snow."
- *osu* = "push/press against."
- *zendō* = "Zen hall/temple."
- *yuki* is "snow," and *-gakoi* is from *kakoi*, "enclosure/fence," so *yukigakoi* = "snow fence."
- *ōyuki ga osu* is a complete thought/sentence ("the heavy snow presses") that can be thought of either as modifying *zendō no yukigakoi* ("the Zen hall's snow fence") or as set off by a colon.

*Other points of interest:*
- Eihei-ji, in Fukui Prefecture, is one of the best known of Japan's Zen temples.

秋の蝶　　生きてゐる黄は　　最も黄
*Aki no chō*　　*ikite-iru ki wa*　　*mottomo ki*

### *The living yellow*
### *of the autumn butterfly —*
### *yellow above all!*

Composed 1972.
In fall the leaves turn yellow. Yellow autumn butterflies flit about.
The yellow of the autumn butterflies is beautiful because it is a living
yellow. Elsewhere I associated the word "living" with the brightness
of the firefly's light.

---

Season Word: *aki no chō*, "autumn butterfly." Autumn, animals.

*Vocabulary:*
- 生きてゐる is the old spelling of 生きている *ikite-iru* ("is alive/living"), which here directly modifies *ki* ("yellow") → "a living yellow."
- *mottomo* means "most," so *mottomo ki* is "most yellow/yellowest."
- *aki no chō* ("the autumn butterfly") is the primary topic of the poem, so *ikiteiru ki wa mottomo ki* means "its living yellow is the most yellow/yellowest of all."

278

放生の　　善為し終へて　　氷張る
*Hōshō no　　zen nashioete　　kōri haru*

## The ceremonies
## of freeing creatures over,
## the ice spreads its sheet.

Composed 1974.
The Sarusawa Pond, in Nara, is used for the living-creature liberation ceremony. It is the place where fish are set free to live their lives and where this year the ceremony has already been observed. The pond is frozen now; the ceremony would be impossible on a frozen pond.

---

Season Word: *kōri*, "ice." Winter, topography.

*Vocabulary:*
- *hōshō* is made up of kanji meaning "release/liberate" and "life."
- 善 *zen* means "goodness/good deed," so *hōshō no zen* literally means "the good deed of liberating life." This refers to a Buddhist ceremony.
- *nashi* is from *nasu*, which is essentially equivalent to *suru* ("do"); in modern Japanese, *nasu* is generally reserved for certain idiomatic and formal uses.
- *-oete* is the *-te* form of the suffix *-oeru* ("finish/complete [something]"); *nashioeru* would mean "finish doing," but since the *-te* form implies a subsequent action, *nashioete* means "after finishing/after [it] was done."
- *haru* means "stretch/spread (across)," or, when speaking of ice, "forms in a sheet/layer."

279

差し出でて　崎々迎ふ　初日の出
*Sashiidete*　*sakizaki mukau*　*hatsu hinode*

*The year's first sunrise —*
*cape after cape standing forth,*
*extending greetings.*

Composed 1974.
The Pearl Road, in Shima. When you look from the mountains at the sea, you can see a number of capes jutting forth. The New Year's sun has just come out of the sea and risen above them. The capes all lean forward to welcome it.

---

✦ Season Word: *hatsu hinode*, "New Year's sunrise." New Year's, celestial phenomena.

*Vocabulary:*
- *sashiidete* is the *-te* form of the classical verb *sashiizu*, which means both "extend [something] forward" and "[something] emerges/comes out." Here, the New Year's sun emerges and the capes extend their tips forward to greet it.
- *saki* = "cape/promontory," and *sakizaki* (the second *s* changes to *z* for euphony) makes it plural.
- 迎ふ *mukau* is the classical form of 迎える *mukaeru* ("welcome/greet/meet"); *sakizaki* is the subject of this verb.
- *hatsu* is used before other words to mean "the first –," and at New Year's, "the first – of the year." *Hinode* = "sunrise," so *hatsu hinode* is literally "the first sunrise of the year."

鴨殘る　　藤村の間に　　藤村も
Kamo nokoru　Tōson no ma ni　Tōson mo

*One duck remaining,*
*in the room where Tōson stayed*
*Tōson, too, remains.*

Composed 1974.
Tōson stayed at the Minami Inn, in Matsue, while writing "A Gift from San'in." The room he occupied has been carefully preserved. When I saw the lone duck remaining on Lake Shinji, it occurred to me that Tōson is still in the room.

◆　Season Word: *kamo*, "duck." Winter, animals.

*Vocabulary:*
- *nokoru* = "remain/stay/linger."
- *ma* means "room," and – *no ma* is the standard way of naming rooms in a traditional Japanese inn — though one does not frequently see rooms named after someone who stayed there.
- *mo* = "too/also," and *Tōson mo* implies "Tōson, too, remains."

*Other points of interest:*
- Shimazaki Tōson (1872–1943) was one of the principal Japanese novelists of the early twentieth century. His best known work is *The Broken Commandment* (*Hakai*), of 1906, a realistic work about a young man coming to terms with his descent from an outcast group.

281

巨き船　出でゆき蜃気　楼となる
Ōki fune　　　ide yuki shinki　　　-rō to naru

*Great ocean liner*
*setting out on a voyage*
*becomes a mirage.*

Composed 1974.
Having been readied for sailing in the shipyard, a great ocean liner stands out to sea. The ocean is hazy, so the liner appears to be a mirage. The place is the Bay of Nago, long reputed to be the site of mirages.

---

✦　Season Word: *shinkirō*, "mirage." Spring, celestial phenomena.

*Vocabulary:*
- *ōki* is the *-ki* form of *ōshi*, one of the classical equivalents for *ōkii* ("large/great"); *ōki fune* = "great boat/ship/ocean liner."
- *ide yuki* is equivalent to *dete itte* ("goes out and . . .") in modern Japanese.
- *. . . to naru* is an expression meaning "becomes . . . ," so *shinkirō to naru* = "becomes a mirage."

# 山脈の　　果の岬に　ちちろ鳴く

*Sanmyaku no　hate no misaki ni　chichiro naku*

## *Where the mountain range resolves itself in a cape, a cricket chirping.*

Composed 1974.
Erimo Point, in Hokkaidō. The mountain range comes down to the sea to form Erimo Point. Standing on the extreme end of the cape, I could hear a cricket chirping faintly. It was at the end of a cape at the end of a mountain range.

---

Season Word: *chichiro*, "cricket." Autumn, animals.

*Vocabulary:*
- *sanmyaku* = "mountain range."
- *hate* = "the end/the farthest point."
- *misaki* = "cape/promontory/point."
- *ni* = "at/on," so *sanmyaku no hate no misaki ni* = "on a cape at the end of a mountain range."
- *naku* = "(an animal) cries/sings/calls" → *chichiro naku* = "cricket chirps."

道路鏡　　雪より鏡　　掘り出され
Dōrokyō　　yuki yori kagami　　horidasare

# *Mirror at the turn —*
# *only its lens shoveled out*
# *of the drifted snow.*

Composed 1974.
When spring came, the road through Mount Hakkōda was plowed open.
When I went along it in a car, I saw that a traffic mirror had been dug out
of the snow. Yet all it reflected was snow. At least it was working.

---

Season Word: *yuki,* "snow." Winter, celestial phenomena.

*Vocabulary:*
- *dōro* = "road/highway," and *kyō* = "mirror," so *dōrokyō* = "road mirror/highway mirror."
- *yori* = "from."
- 鏡 is read *kyō* in combinations but *kagami* when standing alone. In either case it means "mirror/looking glass."
- *horidasare* is a passive form of *horidasu* ("dig out"), from *horu* ("dig") and *dasu* ("take/put out"); *yuki yori horidasare(te-iru)* = "has been dug out from the snow."

284

螢火の　　極限の火は　　緑なる
*Hotarubi no*　*kyokugen no hi wa*　*midori naru*

## *The firefly's light*
## *is green in the period*
## *when it is brightest.*

Composed 1974.
A firefly flew by with its light burning. The light dimmed and bright-
ened, perhaps because of the insect's breathing. The strongest hue was
green; the extreme edge of blue is green.

---

✦   Season Word: *hotarubi*, "firefly's light." Summer, animals.

*Vocabulary:*
- 火 *-bi* (read *hi* when standing alone) = "fire/light," so *hotarubi* = "firefly light."
- *kyokugen* is literally "extreme limit." *Hatarubi no kyokugen no hi* is literally "the light at the extreme limit of the firefly light" → "the brightest point of the firefly light."
- *midori* = "green."
- *naru* is a classical form equivalent to *da/desu* ("is") in modern, so *midori naru* = "is green."

男雛より　女雛宝冠　だけ高し
*Obina yori　mebina hōkan　dake takashi*

*Empress doll on stand,*
*taller than the Emperor*
*by only her crown.*

Composed 1974.
On the doll stand, the Emperor was on the left and the Empress on the right. Their seated figures have the same height, but the Empress is wearing a crown, so she appears taller than the Emperor by the height of her crown.

---

Season Word: *hina*, "festival doll." Spring, observances.

*Vocabulary:*
- *hina* ("festival doll") becomes -*bina* in combinations; *obina* = "male doll," while *mebina* = "female doll"—here referring to the Emperor and Empress dolls.
- *yori* = "more than."
- *hōkan* = "crown," and *hōkan dake* = "only [her] crown."
- *takashi* is the classical "dictionary form" of *takai* ("high/tall"), in this case implying "higher/taller" because of *yori*.

286

梅雨大河　　まさに一級　　河川なる

*Tsuyu taiga*　　*masa-ni ikkyū*　　*kasen naru*

## In rainy season,
## more than ever, this river
## ranks in the first class.

Composed 1974.

The Kiso River, swollen with the early summer rains, has become a great river. Even small rivers are sometimes designated as first-class rivers, but the Kiso River in the rainy season is undeniably first class.

Season Word: *tsuyu*, "rainy season." Summer, celestial phenomena.

*Vocabulary:*
- *taiga* is literally "great river."
- *masa-ni* = "exactly/precisely/truly/indeed": *masa-ni . . . da/desu* would mean "is precisely . . ." or "is indeed . . ."
- *ikkyū* = "first class/rank," and *kasen* is a formal/technical term for "rivers/waterways." *Ikkyū kasen* is an official classification given to major waterways for administrative purposes.
- *naru* is a classical equivalent of *da/desu* ("is"), so *masa-ni ikkyū kasen naru* = "is indeed/ truly a first-rank waterway."

落葉松は　　直幹落葉　　しつくして
Karamatsu wa　　chokukan ochiba　　shitsukushite

*Vertical tree trunks*
　　*with all their needles fallen —*
　　*larches in winter.*

Composed 1974.
The road up Mount Kiso goes through a stand of larches. The trees
are very straight, and with all their foliage gone stand upright and
tall. That vertical quality.

---

Season Word: *ochiba*, "fallen needles." Winter, plants.

*Vocabulary:*
- 落葉松 *karamatsu* ("larch") is written with kanji meaning "fall," "leaf," and "pine" →
  "pine that drops its needles/deciduous pine." All trees of the pine family contain *matsu* in
  their name, and their needles are referred to as 葉 *ha*, the same kanji/word used for the
  leaves of broad-leaved trees.
- *chokukan* is literally "straight trunk." *Karamatsu wa chokukan* = "the larches are straight-
  trunked" → "the larches show their straight trunks."
- *ochiba* is the usual reading for 落葉, "falling/fallen leaves."
- *shitsukushite* is the *-te* form of *shitsukusu*: *shi* is from *suru* ("do"), and *-tsukusu* is a verb
  suffix meaning "[do] fully/completely." *Ochiba* followed by a form of *suru* makes a verb,
  "to drop [its/their] leaves," and *ochiba shitsukushite* means "having fully dropped its/their
  leaves."

288

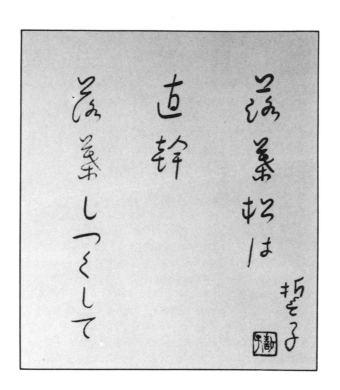

藤蔓折は
直幹
藤蔓してつくして

哲子

北海の　　幹線雪の　　狭軌道
*Hokkai no　　kansen yuki no　　kyōkidō*

## *Hokkaidō trunk line, becoming narrower gauge in the winter snow.*

Composed 1974.
Snowy Hokkaidō. The main train line goes through that snow. It is a narrow-gauge road, and the snow on either side makes it even narrower. Can this be the Hokkaidō Main Line?

---

Season Word: *yuki*, "snow." Winter, celestial phenomena.

*Vocabulary:*
- *Hokkai* here stands for Hokkaidō.
- *kansen* = "trunk line."
- *kyō* means "narrow," and *kidō* means "railroad/train tracks."

親燕　　雷雨の中を　　餌を捕りに

*Oya tsubame*　　*raiu no naka o*　　*e o tori ni*

## *A parent swallow*
## *flies into the thunderstorm*
## *foraging for food.*

Composed 1974.

Hanaze, in the interior of Kurama. A thunderstorm strikes in the
mountainous region. The little swallows in the nests are hungry,
however, so the parents must fly into the storm to get food for them.

---

✦　Season Word: *oya tsubame*, "parent swallow." Summer, animals.

*Vocabulary:*
- *raiu* is made up of kanji for "thunder" and "rain" → "thunderstorm"; *raiu no naka* = "in a/the thunderstorm."
- *e* = "food/feed (for animals)."
- *tori* is from *toru*, "take/get," and *tori ni* implies *tori ni iku*, "goes to get."
- . . . *o iku* means "goes along/through," so with the implied *iku*, the phrase *raiu no naka o* means "(goes) through a thunderstorm."

木曽古道　雪白くして　猶存す
*Kiso kodō*　　*yuki shiroku shite*　　*nao sonsu*

# The Old Kiso Road,
## white beneath the falling snow,
### what it always was.

Composed 1974.
I went from Magome through the pass to Tsumago. A narrow path
branched to the right off the snowy pass. It was white with snow.
That narrow white path was the old Kiso highway, the Nakasendō.

---

Season Word: *yuki*, "snow." Winter, celestial phenomena.

*Vocabulary:*
- *Kiso* refers to an area in Nagano Prefecture.
- *kodō* is literally "old road."
- *yuki shiroku* can be thought of as a single adjective, "whitened by/with snow."
  The expression . . . *shite nao* following an adjective means "is – and yet/but still/
  even so . . ."
- *sonsu* is a classical equivalent of *sonsuru* ("exist"). *Yuki shiroku shite nao sonsu*
  = "[it is] whitened with snow but still there (as it was before)."

*Other points of interest:*
- Nakasendō runs through the Japan Alps of Nagano Prefecture, one of the most
  beautiful and forbiddingly rugged areas of Japan.

雪の道　　木地屋の前は　　木屑道
*Yuki no michi*　　*kijiya no mae wa*　　*kikuzu michi*

*A road under snow*
*running past a carver's shop —*
*call it "Shavings Road."*

Composed 1974.
On the way to Ina from Tsumago is a village of woodcarvers. When I
went to see one of the carvers on that snowy road, the road in front of
his house was littered with shavings, making it a "shavings road."

---

Season Word: *yuki*, "snow." Winter, celestial phenomena.

*Vocabulary:*
- *michi* means "path/road/street"; *yuki no michi* = "snowy/snow-covered road,"
  and *kikuzu michi* = "wood shavings (-covered) road."
- *kijiya* refers to a traditional Japanese craftsman who carves wooden trays/bowls/
  dolls by turning them on a wheel/lathe. The suffix *-ya* can refer either to the
  craftsman himself or to his shop/workshop, so *kijiya no mae* = "in front of the
  carver's shop."

高低の　　雪吊雪に　　蜂起せる
*Takahiku no　yukitsuri yuki ni　　hōki seru*

## Snowy branch supports,
## standing in high and low ranks,
## rise against the snow.

Composed 1975.
The garden of an inn in the snow country. Snow-load supports are used with both high and low trees and thus come in tall and short sizes. They look like poles with pennants.

Season Word: *yukitsuri*, "snowy branch support." Winter, life.

*Vocabulary:*
- *takahiku* is written with kanji meaning "high" and "low," and *takahiku no yukitsuri* means "high and low/tall and short snow branch supports."
- *yuki ni* = "in the snow."
- *hōki seru* is a classical equivalent of *hōki shite-iru*, the progressive form of *hōki suru*, meaning "rise up and swarm about" (the kanji 蜂起 literally mean "bees awaken"). The word is most frequently used in reference to crowds/armies involved in civil disturbances/insurrections.

青リンク　　猿投の姫の　　裳裾なる

*Aorinku*　　　*Sanage no hime no*　　*mosuso naru*

## *This verdant golf course,*
## *the hemline of the garment*
## *of the mountain queen.*

Composed 1975.
The golf course at the base of Mount Sanage. The mountain is sacred
to the memory of Princess Ichikishima, and the green course is the
hem of her garment. Golfers play their game on it.

Season Word: *ao*, "green." Summer, plants.

*Vocabulary:*
- *rinku* is a katakana rendering of English "links," so *aorinku* is "green links/
  green golf course."
- *Sanage no hime* = "the princess of (Mount) Sanage."
- *mo* refers to a kind of "train" worn by court ladies in ancient Japan, and *suso*
  refers to the lower "fringe/hemline" of that train.
- *naru* in classical Japanese can mean either "is/are" or "is located at/on."

*Other points of interest:*
- Princess Ichikishima is mentioned in *Kojiki* ("Record of Ancient Matters," 712),
  the oldest Japanese book extant, as one of three goddesses born from Susanoo's
  sword in his encounter with Amaterasu Ōmikami, the sun goddess.

大寺の　　蓮の葉すべて　　承露盤
Ōdera no　　hasu no ha subete　　shōroban

## *All the lotus leaves*
## *of this great temple function*
## *as dew collectors.*

Composed 1975.

At Senshū-ji, main temple of the Takada sect, in Ise, there is a garden
with a pond. The lotuses have spread their leaves, and dew has
collected on them. Is the term "dew collector" a way of referring to a
lotus with dew on its leaves?

---

Season Word: *hasu*, "lotus." Summer, plants.

*Vocabulary:*
- *ōdera* = "great temple."
- *ha* = "leaf/leaves," so *hasu no ha* = "lotus leaf/leaves."
- *subete* = "all/every one of them."
- the original *shōroban* were basins made of copper that Emperor Wu of the Han
  dynasty in China ordered set out to catch the "heavenly dew of youth/immortal-
  ity."

仏恩に　　浸る銀杏の　　大緑蔭
*Butsuon ni*　　*hitaru ichō no*　　*dairyokuin*

## *The gingko's green shade —*
## *to be steeped in the favor*
## *of holy Buddha.*

Composed 1975.
Beside the memorial hall, there is a great gingko tree, which provides
shade in abundance. I entered that shade, and had the feeling I was
receiving the bounty of Buddha.

---

✦　Season Word: *ryokuin*, "green shade." Summer, plants.

*Vocabulary:*
- *butsu* = "the Buddha," and *butsuon* = "Buddha's favor/beneficence."
- *hitaru* = "[I] steep/soak in."
- *ichō* = "gingko tree."
- *dairyokuin* is literally "great green shade." The kanji for "shade," 蔭, is usually read *kage* when it stands alone, and this word appears in a number of Japanese idioms based on the idea that being in a person's shade — i.e., having him as a master/teacher/boss/etc. — is to receive his bounty and become indebted to him.

落螢　俯伏せのまま　火を点す
*Ochibotaru    utsubuse no mama        hi o tomosu*

# Resting firefly,
## his light turned on even while
## he is on the ground.

Composed 1975.
A firefly lands on the ground and flashes its light. When a firefly
flashes as it flies, it lights the air, but on the ground it lights the earth.

Season Word: *hotaru*, "firefly." Summer, animals.

*Vocabulary:*
- *ochibotaru* is from *ochiru* ("fall/drop") and *hotaru* ("firefly"). The context makes it clear, however, that the firefly has "landed" rather than "fallen" on the ground.
- *utsubuse* = "facing downward," and *no mama* means "remains the same/as is," so *utsubuse no mama* means "remains/remaining face down."
- *hi* = "fire/light."
- *tomosu* = "light (a fire)/turn on (a light)."

落螢　火を点しつつ　土を匐ふ

*Ochibotaru   hi o tomoshi tsutsu   tsuchi o hau*

### *Resting firefly,*
### *crawling about on the ground*
### *with his light aglow.*

Composed 1975.

A firefly was flashing on the ground, then started to crawl about. As it blinked on and off, the ground became alternately brighter and darker.

---

Season Word: *hotaru*, "firefly." Summer, animals.

*Vocabulary:*
- *tomoshi* is from *tomosu* ("light [a fire]/turn on [a light]"), and *tsutsu* after a verb means "while -ing," here implying the action is repeated over and over.
- はふ is the old spelling of はう *hau* ("creep/crawl"). Today it is more common to use the kanji 這う.
- with a motion verb like *hau*, the particle *o* means "along/through," so *tsuchi o hau* = "crawls/creeps along the ground."

七万の　　鐘の字が鳴る　紅葉山
*Shichiman no　　kane no ji ga naru　　momijiyama*

## *Mountain of red leaves,*
## *where seventy thousand words*
## *toll with the great bell.*

Composed 1975.
The entire mountain at Taiun-ji, in Hase, was covered with red
leaves. When I rang the temple bell, its marvelous sound resounded
among the red leaves. On the bell are inscribed the seventy thousand
characters of one of the Buddhist scriptures. That is what makes the
sound so wonderful.

---

✦　Season Word: *momiji*, "red leaves." Autumn, plants.

*Vocabulary:*
- *shichiman* = "seventy thousand."
- *kane* = "bell."
- *ji* = "letter(s)/character(s)" → "word(s)."
- *shichiman no kane no ji* = "the seventy thousand characters/words on the bell,"
  and this entire phrase is the subject of *naru* ("sound/ring/toll"), so the poem liter-
  ally says "the seventy thousand words . . . ring/toll."

# 伊吹山　　他山に雪を　　頒け惜しむ

*Ibukiyama*　　*tazan ni yuki o*　　*wakeoshimu*

*Ibukiyama —*
*reluctant to share her snow*
*with other mountains.*

Composed 1975.

Mount Ibuki is the first in its area to become covered with snow, from top to bottom. Her lower neighbors, however, do not become snowy at all. Mount Ibuki seems reluctant to share her snow with them — the snow she gets from the icy winds out of Siberia.

---

Season Word: *yuki*, "snow." Winter, celestial phenomena.

*Vocabulary:*
- *ta* = "other," and *tazan* = "other mountains."
- *wake* is the stem form of *wakeru* ("divide up/share [with]"), and -o*shimu* connected directly to the stem of another verb means "be reluctant/unwilling to do," so *yuki o wakeoshimu* means "is reluctant to share the snow."

301

登り来し　　仏の天に　　花辛夷
*Nobori kishi　　hotoke no ten ni　　hanakobushi*

## *Having climbed to find*
## *within Buddha's paradise*
## *kobushi blossoms!*

Composed 1976.
The new Hasedera, in Iyo Mishima. At the top of a long stone
staircase is Buddha's paradise. There the pure white flowers of a
magnolia are in blossom — fitting flowers for Buddha's paradise and
for offerings.

---

✦　Season Word: *kobushi*, "magnolia." Spring, plants.

*Vocabulary:*
- *nobori kishi* is equivalent to modern *nobotte kita*, the *-te* form of *noboru* ("climb") and the past form of *kuru* ("come") → "came climbing."
- *hotoke* = "the Buddha," and *ten* = "sky/heaven(s)/paradise," so *hotoke no ten* is "the Buddha's paradise."
- *nobori kishi* is a complete thought/sentence ("[I] came climbing") modifying *hotoke no ten*: "the Buddha's paradise to which I came climbing."
- *ni* makes it "in the paradise . . ."
- *kobushi* is a kind of magnolia (*Magnolia kobus*); *hana kobushi* can be "magnolia blossoms," or it can be more like saying "flowering magnolia."

302

愛の媛の　かんざし桃の　花咲かす

*E no hime no　kanzashi momo no　hana sakasu*

## *Peach trees all in bloom*
## *to make a hair ornament*
## *for the love goddess.*

Composed 1976.
Ehime province is ruled by a goddess. The province makes the peach trees bloom on its mountains to decorate her hair.

---

✦  Season Word: *momo no hana*, "peach blossoms." Spring, plants.

*Vocabulary:*
- 愛の媛の *e no hime no* is a play on the name of 愛媛 Ehime Province/Prefecture. 愛, normally read *ai*, means "love," and 媛 means "princess" (or any young lady of noble birth) → "goddess." Changing Ehime to *e no hime (no)* brings the meaning "princess/goddess of love" explicitly to the surface.
- *kanzashi* = "hair ornament"; Seishi explains in his note that the intended meaning is "for the goddess of love to use as a hair ornament."
- *sakasu* is equivalent to *sakaseru*, the causative form of *saku* ("to bloom/blossom") → "makes/causes to bloom."

303

葉月潮　伊雑の宮を　さしてゆく

*Hazukijio*　*Izō no miya o*　*sashite yuku*

# The tides of August
# coming on a pilgrimage
# to the Izō Shrine.

Composed 1976.

In August the great tides of the Pacific Ocean roll into Matoya Bay and, after passing through a narrow strait, enter the Izō Lagoon. A god is enshrined at the Izō Shrine there, and the great tides come all that way to worship the god.

---

✦　Season Word: *hazukijio*, "August tides." Autumn, topography.

*Vocabulary:*
- *hazuki*, literally "leaf month," was the name of the eighth month on the lunar calendar, which in an average year would begin in mid-September on the Julian calendar. Seishi's note seems to indicate, however, that he is in fact speaking of the eighth month on the Julian calendar, August. Even so the season remains autumn because the seasons in haiku are based on the old lunar calendar, and they begin and end about six and a half weeks earlier, on average, than those by the Julian calendar. Thus, autumn runs from about August 8 to November 6.
- *-jio* is from *shio*, meaning "tide(s)/sea water."
- *miya* = "shrine," so *Izō no miya* = "the Izō Shrine."
- *sashite* is from *sasu* ("point/aim at"); *sashite yuku* means "go toward/head for."

304

島の果　　世の果繁る　この丘が

Shima no hate　yo no hate shigeru　kono oka ga

## *This burgeoning hill*
## *at the end of the island,*
## *the end of the world.*

Composed 1976.
Mabuni Hill, on Okinawa, is the place Ei Shimada died in battle.
Located at the end of the island, it also became the end of the world.
Approaching it, all I can see is a green hill — the hill where
Shimada's life ended.

---

◆　Season Word: *shigeru*, "grow abundantly." Summer, plants.

*Vocabulary:*
- *hate* = "the end/the farthest point," so *shima no hate* = "the end of the island," and *yo no hate* = "the end of the world."
- *shigeru* ("[plants] grow abundantly") modifies *kono oka* ("this hill"), and *ga* marks the entire phrase as the subject, in inverted syntax: *shigeru kono oka ga shima no hate, yo no hate* = "This burgeoning hill is the end of the island, the end of the world."

*Other points of interest:*
- Mabunigaoka, or Mabuni Hill, is the site of a high precipice over which thousands of the defenders of Okinawa were driven to their death in World War II. It is now a war memorial.

湧き出づる　清水も産みの　安らかに
*Waki izuru*　　*shimizu mo umi no*　*yasuraka ni*

*This cool water source,*
*flowing gently as the course*
*of life coming forth.*

Composed 1976.
At the Koyasu Shrine, in Hachiōji, is a pond formed by water that
flows from a nearby rock. The pure water bubbles ever so gently,
never turning stagnant. It is the pure water of easy childbirth.

---

✦　Season Word: *shimizu*, "water source." Summer, topography.

*Vocabulary:*
- *waki izuru* is equivalent to modern *waki deru*, "flow/bubble forth." This modifies *shimizu* ("spring").
- *umi* is from *umu* ("bear/give birth").
- *yasuraka* means "peaceful/calm/gentle" in reference to the spring, and it suggests "easy" in reference to giving birth.
- Koyasu, the name of the shrine Seishi gives in his note, means "easy childbirth."

*Other points of interest:*
- visiting a shrine to pray for a satisfactory childbirth is customary for Japanese pregnant women.

306

如来出て　掌に受け給ふ　枝垂梅
*Nyorai dete*　　*te ni uketamō*　　*shidareume*

*Buddha emerges*
*to receive into his hands*
*weeping plum blossoms.*

Composed 1977.
In front of a temple dedicated to the Dainichi Buddha, a weeping
plum was in bloom. The Dainichi Buddha came out of the temple and
took the blossoms in his hand — the blossoms which had bloomed by
the grace of Dainichi.

---

◆　Season Word: *ume*, "plum." Spring, plants.

*Vocabulary:*
- *nyorai* = "a *tathagata*/a Buddha," including but not limited to the original Buddha.
- *dete* is from *deru* ("emerge/come out"): "comes out and . . ."
- *te* means "hand," but using the kanji 掌 makes it more specific: "palm."
- *uke* is from *ukeru* ("receive/catch/cradle") and 給ふ (strictly speaking, *tamafu*, but pronounced *tamō*), is an honorific suffix.
- *shidare* is written with kanji meaning "branch(es)" and "hang/droop/dangle," so *shidareume* refers to a plum tree whose branches droop like those of a weeping willow → "weeping plum."

307

松の蕊　　群立つ燧　　灘を前
*Matsu no shin*　　*muradatsu Hiuchi*　　*-nada o mae*

# *Newly greening pines*
# *stand bristling beside*
# *the Hiuchi Strait.*

Composed 1977.
The Hiuchi Channel, in the Inland Sea, is a place of turbulent currents. Near the water's edge, the pines wore thick clumps of new needles, sticking up like rows of spears with which to oppose Hiuchi's rough tides.

---

✦　Season Word: *matsu no shin*, "pine stamens (pistils)." Spring, plants.

*Vocabulary:*
- *muradatsu* comes from *mure* ("crowd/throng/herd/flock") and *tatsu* ("stand/ arise"), and means "stand in a crowd/throng"; *matsu no shin muradatsu* ="pine stamens/pistils stand in a crowd."
- *Hiuchinada* = "the Hiuchi Channel."
- *. . . o mae ni* = "with . . . before it/them," so *Hiuchinada o mae ni* is "with the Hiuchi Channel before [them]."

街道の　坂に熟れ柿　灯を点す

*Kaidō no    saka ni uregaki    hi o tomosu*

## *Ripened persimmons —*
## *streetlamps illuminating*
## *the way up the hill.*

Composed 1977.

Magome, in Kiso, is a station on the Nakasendō Highway. I went up a hill on the road and saw a persimmon tree bearing scarlet persimmons. They were like lamps lighting up the road.

---

◆　Season Word: *kaki*, "persimmon." Autumn, plants.

*Vocabulary:*
- *kaidō* = "highway," and *saka* = "hill/slope," so *kaidō no saka ni* = "on a hill on the highway."
- *ure-* is from *ureru* ("become ripe"), and *-gaki* is from *kaki* ("persimmon"; *k* changes to *g* for euphony) → *uregaki* = "ripe persimmon(s)."
- *hi* is "light/lamp," and *tomosu* means "light (a fire)/turn on (a light)," so *uregaki (ga) hi o tomosu* is like "ripe persimmons illumine their lights."

309

鳥威す　　金銀金は　　火に見ゆる
*Tori odosu*　　*kingin kin wa*　　*hi ni miyuru*

## *Field bird repeller,*
## *fashioned in silver and gold —*
## *the gold seems afire.*

Composed 1976.
Strips of gold and silver tape are used in grain fields to scare away
birds. The strips glint as they twist in the wind and keep the sparrows
away. To the human eye, the tape is on fire. That, too, would be
enough to frighten away the sparrows.

---

Season Word: *tori odosu,* "to repel birds." Autumn, life.

*Vocabulary:*
- *tori* = "birds," and *odosu* = "to startle/scare" → "repel."
- *tori odosu* is a complete thought/sentence ("to startle/repel birds") modifying *kingin* ("gold and silver").
- *kin wa* separates the gold from the silver: "as for the gold . . ."
- *. . . ni miyuru* is a classical equivalent of *. . . ni mieru* ("appears/looks like"), so *hi ni miyuru* means "looks like fire" → "seems afire."

枯芝の　　密青芝の　　密のまま

*Kareshiba no　mitsu aoshiba no　mitsu no mama*

## *Withered patch of lawn,*
## *thickly planted grass still thick*
## *as when it was green.*

Composed 1976.
A lawn was thick with green grass because the people taking care of it had planted thickly. When the grass withered, however, it was no less thick. The only difference was that "green" had changed to "withered."

---

Season Word: *kareshiba*, "withered lawn." Winter, plants.

*Vocabulary:*
- *mitsu* means "density/closeness/thickness," so *kareshiba no mitsu* = "the thickness of the withered grass," and *aoshiba no mitsu* = "the thickness of the green grass."
- *no mama* means "remains the same/as it was," so *aoshiba no mitsu no mama* = "remains the same as the thickness of the green grass."

真青に　今も賢治の　青田なり
*Massao ni　ima mo Kenji no　aota nari*

*Rice fields deep in green,*
*all with the same bright verdure*
*as in Kenji's time.*

Composed 1977.
Miyazawa Kenji instructed the farmers of his native Iwate Prefecture
in agriculture. Thanks to his guidance, the rice fields became green.
Even after his death, the rice fields have continued to be green.

Season Word: *aota*, "green rice fields." Summer, topography.

*Vocabulary:*
- まっ *ma* is an intensifying prefix, which when used with colors implies "red as red can be/white as white can be/etc." *Massao* can be either blue or green, here the latter: "green as green can be."
- *ima* = "now," and *ima mo* = "now, too/even now."
- *nari* is a classical equivalent of *da/desu* ("is/are"): *Kenji no aota nari* = "are Kenji's green rice fields."

*Other points of interest:*
- Kenji Miyazawa (1896–1933) was a prolific poet and author of children's stories. He lived an almost ascetic life and showed a great love of nature in his poetry and stories; he was also a devoted advocate of farmers' causes.

峯雲の　　贅肉ロダン　なら削る

*Minegumo no　zeiniku Rodan　　nara kezuru*

## *Rodin would have trimmed these soaring cumulus clouds, with their excess flesh.*

Composed 1977.
Towering cloudbanks stand swollen with clouds, like rotund flesh.
Rodin, the sculptor who paid so much attention to flesh, would have
excised it.

---

Season Word: *minegumo*, "cumulus clouds." Summer, celestial phenomena.

*Vocabulary:*
- *minegumo*, from *mine* ("peak/mountain") and *kumo* ("clouds"), means "great column/tower/bank of clouds."
- *zeiniku* = "excess flesh/fat," so *minegumo no zeiniku* essentially means "the cloudbank's excess fat."
- *Rodan* = "Rodin."
- *– nara* = "if it were –" → *Rodan nara* = "if it were Rodin."
- *kezuru* = "trim/shave/carve away."

手花火の　　火は水にして　　迸る
*Tehanabi no*　　*hi wa mizu ni shite*　　*hotobashiru*

*Hand-held sparkler*
*gushing fiery bubbles —*
*fire is water.*

Composed 1977.

A child's sparkler sputters as it burns. The sparks it sprays forth are fire, true, but they look like water — gushing water.

---

Season Word: *tehanabi*, "sparkler." Summer, life.

*Vocabulary:*
- *tehanabi no hi* = "fire/sparks of a sparkler."
- *mizu* = "water," and *mizu ni shite* = "is water and . . ."
- *hotobashiru* = "spurt/spout/spray/gush"; *mizu ni shite hotobashiru* = "is water and sprays forth."

原始より　　碧海冬も　　色変へず

*Genshi yori*　　*ao-umi fuyu mo*　　*iro kaezu*

## *Green when created,*
## *sea never changing color,*
## *even in winter.*

Composed 1977.

Yorontō Island is a living coral reef. The sea surrounding the island is a lovely emerald green. That color has not changed since the island was created. It does not change even in winter.

---

◆　Season Word: *fuyu*, "winter." Winter, season.

*Vocabulary:*
- *genshi* = "the beginning/creation," and *genshi yori* = "from creation."
- 碧 *ao*, like 青 *ao*, can mean either "blue" or "green." Here, *ao-umi* = "green sea."
- *fuyu mo* = "even in winter."
- *iro* = "color," and *kaezu* is a classical equivalent of *kaenai*, negative form of *kaeru* ("to change"). *Ao-umi fuyu mo iro kaezu* = "the green sea does not change color even in winter."

*Other points of interest:*
- the last two poems of this volume seem to be devout evocations of praise for Seishi's beloved country and its legendary origin in the sun and the eternal sea. Yorontō is a short sea distance north of Okinawa.

315

# 燕にも　　美しき天　紫雲天

*Tsubame ni mo　utsukushiki ten　　shiunten*

## *Even the swallows*
## *have found this sky beautiful —*
## *sky of purple clouds.*

Composed 1978.

The Misaki Peninsula in the Inland Sea is the site of the Urashima fable. The clouds that rose from Urashima Tarō's magic casket were said to culminate in this "purple sky." Flocks of swallows fly about in the sky because it is so beautiful.

---

✦　Season Word: *tsubame*, "swallow." Spring, animals.

*Vocabulary:*
- *tsubame ni mo* = "even to the swallows."
- *utsukushiki* is the classical *-ki* form of *utsukushii* ("beautiful/lovely"), and *tsubame ni mo utsukushiki* is a complete thought/sentence ("is beautiful even to the swallows") modifying *ten* ("sky").
- *shiunten* is literally "purple cloud sky" → "sky of purple clouds."

*Other points of interest:*
- Urashima Tarō was a fisherman who, like Rip Van Winkle, discovered upon returning from three years in the kingdom under the sea that he had been gone much longer. When he opened the casket given him by the sea princess, he was transfigured into an old age.

316

# Bibliography

## Works used in preparing "A Study on Yamaguchi Seishi"

*(The principal repository of books by Yamaguchi Seishi as well as books on him is the library of the Haiku Society of Japan, 3-28-10 Hyakunin-chō, Shinjuku-ku, Tokyo 169 (Tel.: 03-3367-6621).*

### Texts in English

Eliot, T. S. *Selected Prose*. (Peregrine Books, 1965).

Frost, Robert. *Robert Frost: Poetry and Prose*. Eds., Edward Connery Lathem and Lawrance Thompson. (Holt, Rinehart, 1972).

Hulme, T. E. *Speculations*. (Routledge, 1960).

Jones, Peter, ed. *Imagist Poetry*. (Penguin, 1976).

### Texts in Japanese
#### Books by Seishi

Yamaguchi, Seishi. *Selected Poems of Yamaguchi Seishi: Modern Haiku with Notes by Authors Series*, I, 28. (The Association of Haiku Poets, 1979).

_____. *Frozen Harbor (Tōkō)*. (Sojinsha Books, 1932).

_____. *Haiku Bungaku Zenshū: Yamaguchi Seishi Hen*. (Daiichi Shobō, 1937).

_____. *Seishi Haiwa*. (Tokyo Gallery of Fine Arts, 1972).

_____. *Haiku Tensaku Kyōshitsu*. (Tamagawa University Press, 1986).

#### Books on Seishi

Hirahata, Seitō. *Interpretation of Seishi's Best Poems*. (Kadokawa Shoten, 1960).

_____. *Haiku Series: Men and Their Works: Yamaguchi Seishi*. (Ōfūsha, 1966).

Kamitani, Kaoru. *Yamaguchi Seishi to Koten* (Meiji Shoin, 1989).

Kuno, Tetsuo. *Yamaguchi Seishi Oboegaki* (Honami Shoten, 1988).

Kurita, Kiyoshi. *Yamaguchi Seishi*. (Ōfūsha, 1979).

Matsui, Toshihiko, ed. *Yamaguchi Seishi Haiku Jūnikagetsu*. (Ōfūsha, 1987).

#### Books by Shiki

Masaoka, Shiki. *Shiki Zenshū: Dai Yon Kan Haiku Haiwa, Vol. I* (Kōdansha, 1975).

_____. *Shiki Zenshū: Dai Go Kan Haiku Haiwa, Vol. II* (Kōdansha, 1975).

### General Works

Azuma, Kyōzō. *Gendai Haiku no Shuppatsu*. (Kawade Shobō, 1939).

*Bibliography*

Ebara, Taizō, ed. *Kyorai Shō, San Sasshi, Tabine Ron.* (Iwanami Bunko, 1968).

Ōsaka-fu, Naniwa School, eds. *Writing Poems on Japanese Nature,* (Brain Center, 1990).

Takahama, Kyoshi. *Haiku e no Michi.* (Iwanami Shinsho, 1955).

Takahama, Kyoshi and Kawahigashi Hekigotō. *Takahama Kyoshi , Kawahigashi Hekigotō. Meiji Bungaku Zenshū, 56.* (Chikuma Shobō, 1967).

Takahashi, Kenji. *Gendai Haiku Sakka Ron.* (Meiji Shobō, 1940).

## **Periodicals**

*Haiku and Essays,* June, 1987. (Special Issue: *The World of Yamaguchi Seishi* ). (Bokuyōsha).

*Haiku,* November, 1969. (Autobiography and Critical Biography Series—*Yamaguchi Seishi*). (Kadokawa Shoten).

*Haiku Kenkyū,* June, 1971. (Special Issue: *A Yamaguchi Seishi Reader*). (Haiku Kenkyūsha).

*Hototogisu,* October, 1913. (Hototogisu Publishing Co.).

*Tenrō.* June, 1986. (*Tenrō* Haiku Conference).

*Tenrō.* October, 1987. (Yamaguchi Seishi Poem-Stone Issue). (*Tenrō* Haiku Conference).

*Tenrō.* Jan., 1988. (*Tenrō* Haiku Conference).

# Index of First Lines

# Index of Japanese Poems

Index